CRIME IN AMERICA

Conservatives' Approaches toward Criminals, Police, Criminal Justice, and the Opioid Crisis

by Paul Brakke

Author of:

American Justice?,
Cops Aren't Such Bad Guys,
The Price of Justice in America,
Fixing the U.S. Criminal Justice System,
Dealing with Illegal Immigration
and the Opioid Crisis,
The Costly U.S. Prison System,
The Great National Divides

CRIME IN AMERICA

Copyright © 2019 by Paul Brakke

TABLE OF CONTENTS

INTRODUCTION

Crime in America is a compendium of a series of six books I wrote on what's wrong with the criminal justice system and how to fix it. This book summarizes the critical insights of these other books in order to reach the widest possible audience, because one of my reasons for writing this book is I hope to inspire real change.

By way of introduction, I am a biomedical scientist and concerned citizen, not a professional criminologist. But in the past three years, I have done extensive research on this subject, so I guess that makes me a newly minted expert. Many books have been written recently on the subject of crime and incarceration, and I have read a lot on the subject. Most of what I have read was written by liberals and for a professional criminologist audience, so it is too long and full of jargon that is likely to be inscrutable to a more general audience. I hope that this book will help fill that void by summarizing and analyzing conclusions drawn in those books and providing additional insight. I fear that not enough of the public, in particular the conservative public, is aware of the seriousness of the present situation, which calls for quick corrective action, lest we end up with unnecessarily high costs and mounting crime.

As you will see in reading this book, there are serious problems that are continually overlooked. It doesn't matter what side of the political aisle you are on, but there are real failings that are economically costly, lead to the break-up of families, and make America less safe. For example, as this book illustrates, unnecessary incarcerations in prison of individuals who have committed less serious crimes actually leads to more crime and recidivism -- the re-arrest of ex-cons -- while undermining the ability of released prisoners to find jobs and become productive citizens. Their families are often reduced to poverty because the prisoner is out of work.

But as the book describes, for this and other problems I have discussed, there are many things we can do as individuals, along with changes in organizations, local and national legislative changes, and more.

This book is organized into five sections. The first deals with crime, who commits it, and the police as our first line of defense. The second section deals with punishment and its consequences, including the swamped criminal justice system, the positive and negative results of incarceration, and collateral damage to the families of those incarcerated. Suggested remedies are scattered throughout these first two sections, but the third section concentrates on specific solutions, emphasizing lowering recidivism. A fourth section concentrates on our drug plague, and a final section deals with divisions in the nation, some raised in previous sections, that must be healed to make America great again.

I have written this book featuring key points of my other books because the original books are sometimes quite technical, based on extensive research. Some include graphs and charts showing statistical analysis, which help to support my conclusions and recommendations. While criminal justice professionals, academics, and researchers may find these data critical for understanding what's wrong and supporting my suggestions for how to fix the system, others may find this too much detail. I have written this book for a broad general audience more interested in a basic understanding of the problems and my recommendations for fixing them.

Those who are interested can refer to the original books, which contain additional recommendations. These books are:

Dealing with Illegal Immigrants and the Opioid Crisis,
The Price of Justice in America,
Cops Aren't Such Bad Guys,
Fixing the U.S. Criminal Justice System,
The Costly U.S. Prison System,
The Great National Divides

If you have any questions or comments, I welcome your input. You can reach me at brakkep@gmail.com.

PART I: CRIME

- **Who Commits Crime**
- **Police: Our First Line of Defense**

CHAPTER 1: WHO COMMITS CRIME

Some Illegal Immigrants Really Do Commit More Crimes[1]

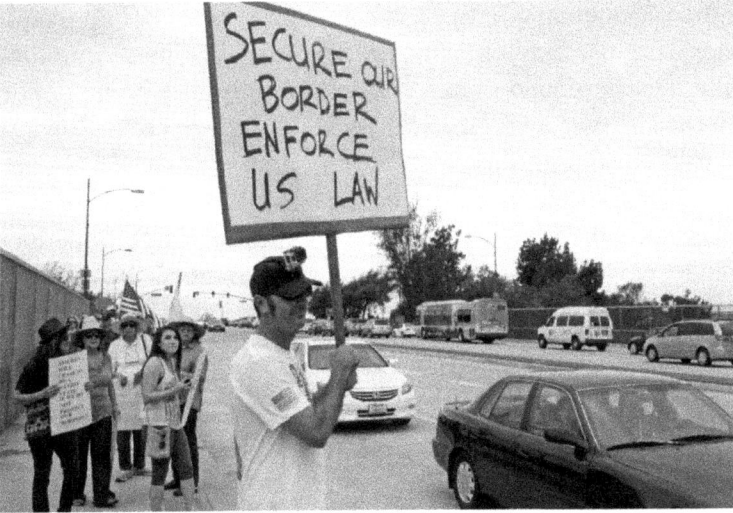

Citizens around the world are revolting against too much immigration. The revolt is especially profound in liberal Western Europe, where populism has become a form of nationalism. The European Union itself could well become a casualty, as evidenced by Brexit, and by increasingly anti-immigrant governments in previously Socialist countries. Each area has its own immigrant problem. The UK has to deal with immigrants from Eastern Europe. The Near East has to deal with immigrants from Syria and Iraq. Europe has to deal with immigrants from there as well as Afghanistan and Africa. Bangladesh has to deal with immigrants from Myanmar. And we have to deal with immigrants from Mexico and Central America.

According to the national and mostly liberal U.S. media, immigrants commit fewer crimes. These statistics have been used to support an agenda that is designed to protect or provide citizenships for the Dreamers, the children of illegal immigrants. A similar argument has been used to support the illegals and prevent their deportation or any action by Federal agents to find and deport illegals. Liberals commonly refer to the illegals as "undocumented" immigrants, just as they have done in setting up so-called "Sanctuary" cities to protect them from being deported. But let's not use euphemisms; let's be clear that these immigrants are illegally here, and therefore they are rightfully being deported when they are discovered. So now let's concentrate on what we need to do deal with the illegal immigrants who should not be here.

Much of the argument of the liberals about the low rate of crime among the illegals is also false or misleading, if one looks more closely at the data. As it turns out, in some states and for some illegal demographic groups, the crime rate is actually higher for more serious crimes, such as robbery, theft, and crimes involving violence. Illegals tend to come from a younger demographic from 16 to 35, which is more prone to crime than older groups. By contrast more settled immigrants are likely to have the lower crime rate frequently attributed to ALL illegal immigrants by the liberals to bolster their argument to keep the illegals here. Thus, a closer look at the data provides support for the government keeping illegals from coming into the U.S. and for being more selective about the immigrants that are permitted to come, such as immigrants who are older, more settled, and well-educated.

In fact, this more limited and selective approach is especially needed now, given that there are now over 65 million refugees around the world, and many of those let into other countries, such as about 1 million let into Germany, have already proved to be a problem for the police there. So just imagine if the U.S. had open doors and just a fraction of these 65 million refugees tried to gain refuge in the United States -- just 10% would be 6.5 million. Obviously that huge number of refugees admitted into the

United States would be very destabilizing, given their problems with finding employment, poverty, differences in languages, and being drawn to crime, given a lack of other opportunities. Lately, the U.S. has allowed an average of about 1 million immigrants in a given year and never more than 2 million.

With those considerations in mind, let's look at some crime stats from Arizona.

A major study about illegal immigrants in Arizona found they had twice the crime rate as other residents, as described by Stephen Dinan in a *Washington Times* article: "Illegals Commit Crimes at Double the Rate of Native-Born: Study."[2] The report was issued by the Crime Prevention Research Center, and it used a previously untapped source of data from Arizona which examined criminal convictions. Among other things the study found that illegal immigrants between 15 and 35 represented less than 3% of the state's population, but they made up nearly 8% of its prison population. Moreover, the crimes they were convicted for were generally more serious than just being illegal immigrants. As the author of the report and president of the research center, John R. Lott Jr. pointed out, using the term "undocumented" to refer to illegal immigrants:

> "There appears to be a huge difference between the two groups. The type of person who goes through the process to legally immigrate to the United States appears to be very law-abiding versus even the U.S.-born population. The reverse is true for undocumented immigrants -- they are committing crimes, and more serious crimes."

Lott also pointed out that among the nearly 4000 first and second-degree murder convictions, the distinction between the legal and illegal immigrants was huge. Whereas the legal immigrants represented less than 1% of the prisoners convicted of murder, the illegal immigrants represented nearly 13%.

He also noted that illegal immigrants had five times the rate of convictions for money-laundering and kidnapping, and they were three times more likely to have convictions for drive-by-shootings.

Moreover, Lott emphasized that the crime-rate for illegal immigrants in the 18 to 35 year old group was especially significant. He pointed out that the data from Arizona suggested that the illegals' crime rate was 250% higher than might be predicted by their percentage of the population.

In commenting on this report, Attorney General Sessions pointed out that the illegal immigrants were more likely to be convicted of sexual assault, robbery and driving under the influence. In fact, as he observed: "Tens of thousands of crimes have been committed in this country that would never have happened if our immigration laws were enforced and respected like they ought to be."

Certainly, we have plenty of crimes by legal residents -- too many crimes, as everyone would agree. But we don't need to have even more crimes committed by illegal immigrants, who have now been shown to commit a disproportionate share of crimes. And certainly, if a study of statistics in Arizona could show such dramatic differences, it seems likely that similar studies in other states might reflect a similar pattern.

In the next sections, I'll discuss the crimes committed by illegal immigrants, most of whom are Hispanics, and what to do about the illegal immigration problem.

Some of the Serious Crimes Committed by Illegal Immigrants[3]

Probably the most well-known recent case involving an illegal immigrant and a violent crime involves the killing of Kate Steinle in San Francisco. This occurred when Jose Ines Garcia Zarate shot her on a pier with a stolen gun he claims he found there that went off accidentally. It is true that the jury bought his argument that this was an accident based on the bullet ricocheting on the ground before it killed her. But he was later found guilty of felony possession of a gun, whether he stole it or not. Had he been turned over by the San Francisco Sheriff's Department to the Federal Immigration authorities, who would have deported him because of his extensive prior convictions and his repeated returns to the Bay Area. Then he would not have been on the pier, and Kate Steinle would not have been shot. In short, Kate Steinle's death is one that didn't have to happen, and it only happened because an illegal immigrant remained in the United States, rather than being deported, due to San Francisco sanctuary city policies, which remain in effect today.

Certainly, as liberals may argue in support of keeping illegal immigrants here, there are many similarly serious crimes committed by native born and legal immigrants. And that's true. There are. But that's not the point. What is important is that these are *additional* crimes by illegals that wouldn't have happened if they weren't permitted to come to the United States or stay here.

To make another point: we taxpayers are paying for their prison stays.[4]

Hispanics Commit More Violent Crime than Whites[5]

Hispanics commit considerably more crimes than whites. Here's how I reached this conclusion through a careful analysis of crime statistics.

Violent crime statistics are available for blacks, whites and Hispanics.[6] As with any type of killing, violent crime victims and their offenders primarily occur within the same racial or ethnic group. Thus, white offenders are the main perpetrators of violent crimes against white victims; black offenders the main perpetrators of such crimes against black victims; and the same holds true for Hispanics. More specifically, where the racial or ethnicity of the offenders was known, 56.6% of the violent crimes against white victims were committed by white offenders, whereas only 14.7% of these crimes involved black offenders and 11.0% involved Hispanic offenders. The totals don't add up to 100% because the racial and ethnic identity was not known in almost 20% of the cases for a variety of reasons. After setting aside that 20%, here's why the Hispanics' crime rate is higher.

Between 2012 and 2015, the average number of whites, blacks, and Hispanic 12 or older in the U.S. was as follows:

Whites: 172,611,780
Blacks: 32,599,700
Hispanics: 41,364,400.

During the same time period, the victims of violent crime were as follows:

3,679,410 white victims annually
56.6% committed by white offenders
14.7% committed by black offenders
11.0% committed by Hispanic offenders
17.7% committed by persons of unknown race/ethnicity
850,720 black victims annually
10.9% committed by white offenders
63.2% committed by black offenders
6.6% committed by Hispanic offenders
19.3% committed by persons of unknown race/ethnicity
846,520 Hispanic victims annually
20.0% committed by white offenders
20.5% committed by black offenders
40.3% committed by Hispanic offenders
19.2% committed by persons of unknown race/ethnicity

The table below compares the rate of violent crimes committed per individual of each race/ethnicity.

	White victims	Black victims	Hispanic victims	All victims
White offenders	12.1	0.5	1.0	13.6
Black offenders	16.6	16.5	5.3	38.4
Hispanic offenders	9.8	1.4	8.2	19.4
All offenders[7]	--	--	--	--

The results couldn't be clearer. As the table indicates, per capita, blacks commit the most violent crime (38.4), while Hispanics commit only about half as much (19.4), but still considerably more than whites (13.6).

The extent of Hispanic participation in violent crime is less well-known than that of blacks. However, their relatively high rate of violent crime against mostly white and Hispanic victims is important new information for law enforcement and legislators to know in dealing with Hispanic perpetrators. This higher propensity for violence is also why there is a much higher percentage of Hispanics in prison than whites.[8]

This information about the criminality of Hispanics also puts the lie to the liberal contention that immigrants do not contribute to crime. Rather this data analysis indicates that Hispanics do commit more violent crime than whites, especially against both whites and other Hispanics. Moreover, it seems most likely that the Hispanics committing these violent crimes are illegal immigrants, since they commit more violent crime than Hispanics who are legal immigrants or long-established citizens. This is because a much higher percentage of illegal immigrants are in the 18-39 age group compared to the general population of Hispanic Americans, and this younger group commits far more violent crimes than other age groups.

The data analysis in the above table also shows that Hispanic offenders are even more likely to target whites than Hispanics, and that black offenders are equally prone to selecting white victims as black ones.

These results present troubling news for their potential white victims. Indeed, this analysis shows that whites have the highest rate of being victimized by all groups.[9] Much has been made of black-on-black and Hispanic-on-Hispanic crime, but these data suggest that the law-abiding white community has as much to fear from these minorities as it does from white criminals. No wonder white suburban housewives are especially fearful of falling victim to these groups.

Still, Hispanics have the most to fear from other Hispanics, since illegal immigrants exhibit higher violent crime rates than other Hispanics. As a result, law-abiding Hispanics should be encouraged to report illegals to the authorities in order to increase their own safety.

Some Suggestions for Fixing the Illegal Immigrant Mess[10]

The younger more recent illegal immigrants are the prime offenders, since just by virtue of their youth, they are more likely to get involved in crime, as well as participate in the gang activity of the many gangs made up primarily of illegal immigrants, such as MS-13.

Therefore, something must be done to deal with this problem and find some solutions to both reduce illegal immigration and the crimes the illegal immigrants are involved with.

Following are my top 3 of 6 recommendations from this section of my book *Dealing with Crime by Illegal Immigrants and the Opioid Crisis*:

1. **Secure the border.** Even though liberals claim that there is a net migration back to Mexico, there are still bad hombres entering along with others illegals to improve their lives and those of their families. An 1800 mile-long concrete wall may not be the answer, but some combination of walls, fences, greater patrols,

drones, and more border security agents is. These different methods should all be used to provide additional security at the possible entry points for illegal immigrants.

This border security should also include having a check for passports or other entry documents at airports for international flights and highways from Mexico and Canada. These checks should incorporate additional checks on the validity of the documents provided, such as fingerprint checks or eye retina scans. Border security agents should tighten up the other ways that illegal immigrants might get into the country, such as by boats to the East and West Coast, tunnels from Mexico, and land journeys through the back country. While walls might work in some areas, illegals might still come through tunnels, rivers, or other natural points of entry, where the terrain doesn't permit walls. Accordingly, more efforts should be made to look for and block tunnels and use drones to look for parties of illegal immigrants trying to get into the United States by land or water.

2. **Discourage illegal immigration** by eliminating the access of illegal immigrants to most services provided by city, state, or local governments. This may even lead many such immigrants to leave the country voluntarily. This will also reduce the high cost of having to locate and deport millions of illegal immigrants, estimated to be about 11 million around the U.S. Such services might include drivers' licenses, health benefits, education, and the like. Should illegal immigrants already have access to benefits, these could be cancelled or they might be prevented from renewing their access, whichever policy is more efficient for the relevant agency.

3. **Institute strict penalties and deportations for crimes committed by illegal immigrants.** These policies should be instituted both to promote public safety by getting illegals committing serious crimes off the street and a deterrent to potential criminals. In the event an illegal is arrested, he or should be subjected to a no-bail condition prior to a trial, and be given the

option of leaving the country through self-deportation or risking harsh penalties as well as deportation if found guilty. Those deported due to criminal activity should be tagged with implantable microchips so that they can be more readily identified if they attempt re-entry to the U.S.

Now that I've given you an overview of the illegal immigration problem in America which incidentally pointed out that blacks commit even more violent crime than Hispanics, here's the truth which the media and liberals don't tell you about homicide patterns for blacks and whites.

The Real Truth about Black and White Homicide Rates in America[11]

Recently, the shootings of blacks by police and the retaliatory shootings of the police by blacks around the U.S. has become a crisis. Certainly there is very little justification for killings of unarmed citizens by police. The only justification is whether the police officer is concerned that his or her own life might be in jeopardy when making a split-second decision about whether to shoot or not. The Black Lives Matter movement has been swift to condemn individual police shootings of blacks and to organize protests. An All Lives Matter movement has arisen in response to say that every life should be treated as worthwhile. Both sides have their points, but they don't seem to try to reconcile these perspectives to arrive at any consensus about what should be done.

What do the homicide statistics show? When I looked at these homicide statistics, I found a number of shocking facts.

Five Key Truths about Homicide Patterns in America

First and foremost, 1.4 million deaths by firearm occurred between 1968 and 2011, a horrible number by any account. However, this number of deaths is not the worst in the world. Our per capita homicide rate is not as bad as that of Russia, Mexico, or many Central American, South American or African countries.

Second, what isn't widely known given the media emphasis on reporting murders is that guns account for more suicides than homicides. Out of 33,000 annual deaths caused by guns, 22,000 were suicides, about two-thirds of the deaths by guns, while only 8600 were homicides. Another 2500 were accidents or unintentional.

Third, crime statistics show that the vast majority of homicides do not involve assault weapons, even though the police may fear being overwhelmed by the firepower of mass murderers. Over 70% of homicides involve handguns, the very weapon most commonly chosen to protect households from break-ins. Citizens in high crime areas would rebuff any attempt to impose restrictions on their ability to defend themselves. Therefore, restricting handguns is not likely to be an option to reduce homicides either. In any case, gun ownership in households has actually declined since 1977, from 50% down to 31% as of 2014, and a far greater proportion of households in rural America possess guns (56%) than urban Americans living in large metropolitan areas (16%) with higher crime statistics.

Fourth, in 2014 more murderers were male (4878 or 90%) than female (543 or 10%); just as more murder victims were male (3976 or 70%) than female (1679 or 30%). So murders are mostly males killing males. At the same time, women are three times more likely to be murder victims than murderers.

Fifth, it appears that most homicides occur within racial groups, so that most whites are killed by whites and most blacks are killed by blacks. As the statistics show, in 2014, 2488 of 3021 or 82% white gun homicide victims were killed by whites or Hispanics, while 2205 of 2451 or 90% of black gun homicide victims were killed by blacks. By contrast, only 18% of black homicide victims were killed by whites. Blacks are the true victims, since proportionate to their population, they are 4 times more likely to be murdered than everyone else, and 6.6 times more likely to be killed than whites.

Some Startling Conclusions about Homicide in America

Thus the statistics show that the overwhelming majority of African American homicides are perpetrated by other blacks. Only a very small proportion of black killings are carried out by whites, though certainly such killings should be condemned and reduced, too. Only a truly tiny proportion of black killings are due to the police, though the media and Black Lives Matter movement have made these seem much more frequent and due to out of control police bias against blacks than is really the case.

Similarly, only a very small proportion of white killings are carried out by blacks, and most white deaths are due to white on white crime, with negligible involvement by the police. Maybe that's because we still live in a very segregated society. But, whatever the reason, the key point to recognize is that since most blacks are killed by other blacks, and very few by the police. Therefore, the Black Lives Matter movement could save far more black lives by looking at making changes within the communities where most blacks live. Doing so will stem one of the major sources of black on black homicides – gang wars and conflicts between gangs.

While statistics on gang related homicide are hard to come by, it has been estimated that nearly half of all violent crime is committed by gangs, and much more than that in certain large cities. Thus, gang violence is a major factor contributing to the high black and black homicide rate. Therefore, an approach of improving the inner city communities where blacks are concentrated and most of these homicides occur could help to provide a more realistic solution to reducing the carnage than solely placing the blame on racial bias by the police.

How Bad Are Black Homicide Rates?[12]

What is the relationship between homicide statistics and other factors, such as the state of residence, gun ownership, the percentage of blacks in each state, and the median income or incidence of poverty in that state? Homicide statistics are most closely correlated with the percentage of African-Americans in that state and with lower incomes, possibly because living in a lower income community can lead one into crime when jobs and money are scarce. More specifically, here's what I found.

The Major Correlations

- There was no correlation between homicide rates and gun ownership, so owning guns doesn't increase the chance of killing someone or being killed – statistics that Second Amendment supporters appreciate.
- Homicide rates for not only blacks but for all Americans are correlated with the percentage of African Americans in each state. Since homicide rates are highest for blacks, black homicides don't just affect blacks, they also contribute significantly (and disproportionately) to homicide statistics for the entire population.
- There was a correlation, albeit a weaker one, between homicide rates and the median income in each state. Higher homicide rates accompanied *lower* median income. A likely reason is that poverty leads to crime, since the criminals seek to generate income when jobs are scarce. Being impoverished can lead individuals to turn to illegal means of making money, such as drugs. Engaging in these illegal activities can contribute to higher homicide rates due to the growth of gangs as business enterprises running these activities, especially selling drugs. A high crime rate

might in turn contribute to lower income in an area, due to the flight of middle income individuals, both white and black, from a high crime community, contributing to further poverty and crime in these areas.

Correlations by state might also have regional explanations apart from the problem of urban violence, in that inner city homicide and crime rates are the highest. As a candidate, President Trump proclaimed that the African American community never had it so bad in the inner cities and that Democrats had done little to alleviate their plight, so what did they have to lose by supporting him? Though Trump convinced very few blacks to switch their vote to him, he did have a good point in that their situation was now so bad that something had to change for things to get better for them.

Since the data from the states does not distinguish between the homicide rates in inner cities and the rest of the country, I examined FBI and census statistics from 2008-2010 to obtain statistics from over 3000 individual counties nationwide. I assumed that counties with a population under 50,000 were rural counties and that urban counties had populations greater than 50,000. Since the number of homicides in many rural counties was zero, I used statistics on violent crime, including homicides, along with robberies, rape, attempted murder, and battery, for a comparison.

- There was a correlation between violent crime rates and the percentage of black residents in each county in 39 of 50 states, meaning that the violent crime rates were higher when the community had a higher percentage of black residents.

- The correlation was weaker in more rural counties with a population under 50,000, and less than half of the 44 states analyzed showed a correlation in rural counties between the percentage of black residents and violent crime rates.

- The correlation between a high rate of violent crime and the percentage of blacks was stronger in urban counties with a population over 50,000, and two-thirds of the states analyzed showed such a correlation. More than half of the states that showed a correlation showed a strong correlation.

What These Correlations Show about Crime

In short, violent crime and most probably homicide rates correlate highly with the percentage of blacks in the population, especially in U.S. cities. Does crime lead to the increased urban black population? Or does the increased urban black population lead to high crime? Unfortunately, both factors are likely to contribute to what has become a downward spiral for our cities. Violent crime is likely to have caused an increase in the urban black population, because it has led to the flight of middle class whites and blacks to suburban areas with lower crime rates. Though it is politically incorrect to say this, it is even more likely that an increase in the urban black population has led to more violent crime due to their higher rate of low incomes and poverty. In turn, this higher rate is due in part to their lower level of education, higher unemployment rate, and employment in lower paying jobs.

The high rate of crime, violence, and homicide does not seem to accompany middle and upper income blacks who move out of low income, high crime areas. Therefore, the increase in crime in predominantly black urban areas is probably due to the conditions affecting black lives, such as low income, impoverished families, poor education, poor housing, and living in an environment of gangs and drug wars, as discussed next.

Why Are Urban Blacks Associated with Violent Crime?[13]

As the forgoing analysis has shown, most blacks were killed by other blacks, far more than by police, and that blacks killed comparatively few whites, and I'll present more statistics on this in the next chapter. Gun ownership did not correlate with homicide statistics in different states, but the percentage of blacks in the population did, and the correlation of black residence with violent crime was strongest in urban counties. States with lower median income also had higher homicide statistics. Thus, there seemed to be a possible correlation between the high homicide rates of blacks and poverty.

Reasons for the Results

What are the reasons for these correlations? Probably the most likely reason for the correlation of a high incidence of blacks living in an area with violent crime is the high rate of poverty. Many blacks left the South and moved north, most migrating to cities because that's where the jobs were. But there they had to accept lower income jobs because of their inability to obtain higher income jobs, due to discrimination, their lesser education, or lower skill level. The cities were also quite segregated, which may have contributed to the prevalence of black on black crime. Another likely contribution to the correlation between violent crime and poverty was middle class flight from areas of high crime, contributing to increased urban poverty.

Undoubtedly, several factors contribute to the higher correlations of urban blacks and poverty. One consequence of segregation has been to generate black ghettos in certain inner city areas, made all the worse by high unemployment among young black males and the poverty endured by single black moms. It is highly unlikely that single moms are responsible for much of the violent crime correlated with the black community. More likely, the high unemployment rate of young black males is a much bigger factor. Still another possible contribution to the higher correlation of violent crime with urban black poverty may be that it is generally less expensive to live in the countryside on a poverty income than in a city, resulting in less incentive to commit crime to get money to support oneself or one's family. Furthermore, there are likely fewer rural opportunities for participating in an illegal underground economy which includes drugs, "protection" or prostitution.

CHAPTER 2: POLICE: OUR FIRST LINE OF DEFENSE

All Lives Matter

The Rev. Al Sharpton shows up at most Black Lives Matter demonstrations involving the killing of an unarmed black by police, and that heightens media attention. I say ALL LIVES MATTER. Let me explain. While it is true that EVERY LIFE MATTERS, it is also possible to draw too much attention to individual cases, particularly ones that appear to be exceptions to the rule. In contrast, statistics can reveal a more important story.

The fewest fatalities are those of Cops (143 in 2016, only 66 of whom were shot and killed; 128 in 2017, only 44 of whom were shot and killed).[14] But since there are fewer cops than blacks or Hispanics, they suffer the greatest proportion of fatalities at the hands of civilians. As of 2012, there were 1,076,054 police officers,[15] which would mean as a most conservative estimate that there were 41 killings of police per million police. Police officers' lives are on the line every day they serve us. So I certainly agree that BLUE LIVES MATTER.

Next in line, there are more killings of blacks by police officers than there are killings of police. This is the whole basis of the BLACK LIVES MATTER movement. In 2017, police killed 1129 people, of which 25% were black compared to only 13% blacks in the population.[16] Liberals proclaim that disparity indicates racist police action. While there were more killings of blacks by police (282) than there are killings of police, there are a lot more blacks (over 43 million in 2017)[17], so proportionately there are far less killings of blacks by police than there are killings of police, only about 6.5 killings of blacks by police per million blacks. And many of these may have been committing serious life-threatening crimes at the time.

A greater reason for the high number of black deaths is there are far more black-on-black killings than there are black killings by police. The BLACK LIVES MATTER movement ought to pay at least as much attention to that as they do their "mistreatment" by police. This is by far the greatest threat to lives in proportion to their population. In 2015, 2380 blacks were killed by blacks in the 39% of cases where the findings could be substantiated.[18] Assuming those 39% were representative, this would mean that 6105 blacks were killed by blacks, or 142 black-on-black killings per million blacks.

White-on-black killings are far less than black-on-black killings.[19] The statistics suggest there are 30 white-on-black killings per million blacks. These are, however, more significant than the 6.5 killings of blacks by police per million blacks.

Killings of whites by police are small,[20] and so are killings of whites by blacks. So these are also of lesser consequence in affecting the statistical patterns. In 2015, 500 whites were killed by blacks in the 39% of cases that could be substantiated. This translates to 5.2 black-on-white killings per million whites.

White-on-white killing is a larger problem. In 2015, 2574 whites were killed by whites in the 39% of cases that could be substantiated.[21] That translates to 26.7 white-on-white killings per million whites.

Unfortunately, Hispanics were primarily counted as either whites or blacks in these statistics, so I have been unable to ascertain where they fit in. Most likely their homicides are perpetrated primarily by other Hispanics and fall somewhere between the rates of black homicide and those of white homicide. So let's summarize what we've found per million victims:

Killings per million blacks or whites

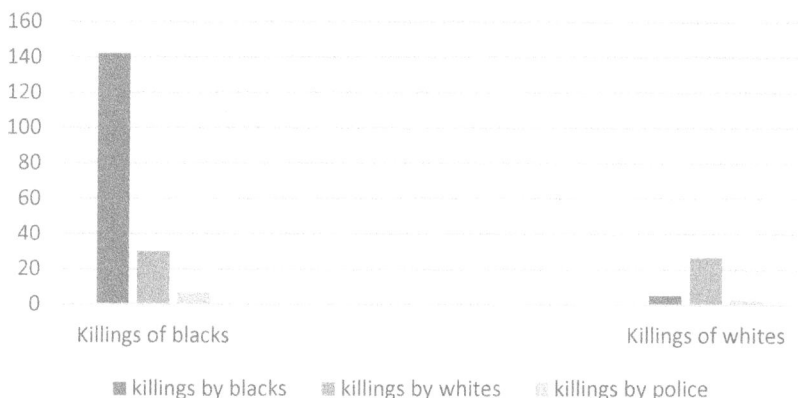

142 black-on-black killings <u>per million blacks</u>
41 killings of police per million police
30 white-on-black killings <u>per million blacks</u>
26.7 white-on-white killings per million whites
6.5 killings of blacks by police <u>per million blacks</u>
5.2 black-on-white killings per million whites
2.5 killings of whites by police per million whites

What's the bottom line here for the BLACK LIVES MATTER movement? It should be abundantly clear that they and Reverend Al should be concentrating on black-on-black killings first, then on killings of blacks by whites, and paying less attention to individual killings of blacks by police that appear to be undeserved.

Is there any bottom line message for whites? It should be that they are far less likely to be killed by blacks than by other whites. That is in contradistinction to the fear of blacks that many whites feel.

Whites, however, should also take home the message that police are dying at the hands of perpetrators at numbers that are far too high, and overall police fatalities in the line of duty raise that number roughly three-fold, several times the average for white-on-white killings. Some policy changes should be implemented to make their jobs safer. I suggest:

Since as many police officers die in traffic incidents as die in shootings[1], and since the traffic stop is potentially very dangerous for both police and stopped driver:

- Do not indulge in high speed chases. Instead inform other units that could intercept the speeding vehicle.
- Issue traffic citations by mail utilizing license plate numbers instead of stopping the car to write out a ticket.

Finally, as a gesture to Reverend Al and the black community:

- any police officer involved in an unnecessary killing of a suspect, even if cleared of wrongdoing, should no longer be permitted to be a beat cop, but should instead be assigned a desk job.
- Furthermore, police procedures regarding the use of deadly force should be revised. There have been too many shootings of unarmed blacks by police, and almost inevitably the acquittal of the police officers involved has been due to the fact that the officers followed local protocols.[22] These protocols and training need to be revised and standardized, at the state level or even nationally, so as to reduce the prevalence of unnecessary killings by police. Police have every reason to fear being shot or stabbed themselves during an apprehension, and they rarely have any way of ascertaining whether the suspect is armed or not.
- If mace, pepper spray or taser could disable the suspect, perhaps that should be used first in certain circumstances.

<u>Reflections on Racism in America</u>[23]

Let's face it. Racisim has been a continuing problem in America, from the days of slavery to today. One result of this continued treatment of most blacks as second class citizens, is continued resentment which occasionally boils over into a confrontation – whether it's one angry black man raging at a white man or a group of angry blacks joining together to protest, loot, trash, or otherwise attack property in the neighborhood.

<u>The Fears Underlying Racism</u>

In turn, many whites fear blacks. This fear wasn't much of a worry during slavery, when black subjugation was total. It has become more of an issue since then, with other forms of subjugation such as lynching, which lasted another 50 years, followed by a period of intense segregation. Desegregation was never very successful and in fact promoted white flight from the inner cities to the suburbs, leaving the inner cities to become cauldrons of crime involving economically distressed blacks and hispanics.

Whites haven't been too concerned about black-on-black crime, including murder, as long as it didn't spill over into their communities. Police became viewed as the first line of defense to keep whites safe from black crime. Yet the mostly white police had to deal with this crime, risking their lives on the front lines of racial tension. Mostly they did this in minority communities where they often weren't wanted or appreciated, because their tactics were often discriminatory or led to discriminatory consequences.

A prime example is when a police officer is quick to suspect an African American man who happened to be within a few blocks of where a crime occurred. So the black man becomes a prime suspect whether he closely fits the description of the suspect or not. He was black, too, wasn't he, and the witness could easily have been mistaken, so the police officer's thinking might go. So the innocent black man is soon arrested, and once in the system, he is often misidentified as the perpetrator of the crime and within a few months, convicted of a crime he didn't do.

Another key reason for this miscarriage of justice is by having less job opportunities and living in the inner city, the black man doesn't have the money to get bail or hire a good defense lawyer. Then the system too readily gobbles him up and he joins the disproportionately black prison population, when his only real crime, so to speak, may be being "black in America." As such, he is more likely to be poor, unemployed, and living in an inner city in an enviroment where drugs, crime, and despair can be found on most city streets everyday.

Periodically, the situation where blacks were continually disadvantaged boiled over into race riots, such as in the sixties. This brought more fear to whites, and the criminal justice system responded with more and more severe sentencing, ballooning the prison system and its associated costs. Some attempts at reform have been implemented locally, such as more community involvement by police, but if the police don't actually live in the neighborhoods they police, it is difficult for them to be accepted by those communities.

Thus, racial tension has continued to be a problem in this country. Witness the events of the past few years which include these killings:

- the shooting by the cops of Michael Brown in Ferguson, Missouri and Walter Scott in Charleston, South Carolina,
- the death of Freddie Gray in a police van in Baltimore, Maryland,
- the killings of Philando Castille in St. Paul, Minnesota and Alton Steele in Baton Rouge, Louisiana,
- and most recently the ambush shooting of cops by Micah Johnson in Dallas, Texas.

After a while, the names of the victims and the killers blend together and may be forgotten, with just the city names as monuments to the days of rage and destruction.

For the most part the killings have been done by cops, though recently more and more cops are being killed. While there may be many factors at play in causing these killings, a continuing theme is the feelings of anger and fear of the other. The police suspect the black man as up to no good and are more prone to shoot first rather than considering any alternatives, while some angry and alienated black men have been influenced by feelings of injustice to strike back in what is often a certain death following their act.

But even though these are killings by individuals, it would be a big mistake to attribute the actions of a few rogue police or blacks to police or blacks generally. Rather, there is no denying that racial tension contributes to the impetus for these killings. And currently, that tension has come to a head in the face-off between cops and African-Americans, whether individual cops and blacks are fighting each other or African-American protesters are sharing their anger with the world. Plus now a growing movement to support the cops – Blue Lives Matter – has emerged from the ashes of the recent cop killing in Dallas.

The media often are complicit in tensions, because they contribute to whipping up attention to conflicts. But so are whites who are content to let the situation fester as long as it doesn't directly affect them. Or they go for simple solutions, such as seeking a crackdown based on the slogan: "Let's not get soft on crime!" But they don't realize that the situation is complex, and a crackdown by itself will only provoke more resistance and fiercer battles.

Fixing the System

So, what's the fix? Clearly, just as there's no single cause, there's no one single fix. The situation has festered for decades and only gotten worse. The numbers are truly appalling. According to data from the U.S. Department of Prisons, FBI, Pew Research, and other sources, about 2 million Americans are in federal, state, and county prisons and jails around the country, and the racial disparities are striking. Black men are six times more likely than white men to be in prison, while Hispanic men are 2.4 times more likely to be there. Moreover, 1 out of 31 Americans are under U.S. corrections custody either through parole, probation, or incarceration, and one in three Americans have a criminal record.

But we need to do something, before the racial divide becomes even greater. A comprehensive plan for criminal justice reform is one place to start, and that's what I call for in my book *American Justice?*. In these divisive, partisan times, it just could be that this is one issue that conservatives concerned about cost and liberals/progressives concerned about discrimination can finally get together in a long-overdue bipartisan manner to regain some public confidence in Washington, DC.

However, not just lawmakers need to get involved. The public has to get involved as well, and push the lawmakers into action. A national dialogue is called for, where both sides acknowledge their contribution to this sad state of affairs. Instead of pointing fingers to lay blame on the other side for what they allegedly did wrong, individuals on both sides of the issue or the aisle need to listen to one another more, whereby they try to understand how difficult things are for those on the other side.

Racial tension is unlikely to go away anytime soon by legislation alone. But we can embark on a path where it can slowly wind down and recede if there is enough public will to address the root causes of this racial tension. A key part of this solution is to see things from the perspective of the other side and then try to reform matters.

The first step is to become more aware of the way the criminal justice system works. The police and blacks are certainly aware of how it usually operates, but they are often intimidated and scared when they confront each other in any situation, such as when a police officer stops a car for a traffic violation. What may seem routine when a police officer stops a white driver, whether for a broken tail light, lack of registration, improperly changing lanes or speeding, is fraught with the potential for violence when an officer stops a car with a black driver or passenger. While the police officer may be fearing the black man may have a gun and reach for it to retaliate, the black man is already thinking about the other black men shot by the police and worried if he might be next if he makes the slightest wrong move. So a simple stop is anything but that.

Whites who don't encounter the system have to educate themselves about how the system really operates on others who are affected by it everyday, especially in the inner city. Whites have to realize the kind of monstrosity this system has become for inner city residents and recognize their own role in creating this system which may operate well for them but has disastrous consequences for others. We all need to realize what is going on before anyone can hope to reform or fix the system with a goal of ending the division and the fear it brings. So now it's time to start before the monster of a system we have created gets any worse!

Overcoming the Police-Citizen Divide[24]

The Number of Citizens Killed by the Police

In the last decade, the police killed many thousand citizens, and often these were individuals of color, a great many in the inner cities. That's because in these confrontations, the police approach the suspect with a siege mentality, given the already hostile relationships between the police and the community in these areas. Thus, they are more ready to feel threatened and shoot, whereas if they encounter a white man who is mentally disturbed or drunk, they are more likely to try to talk to him and defuse the situation.

In turn, such shootings of people of color have contributed to even more hostility to the police in the inner city and among African Americans – and to still more headlines, inflaming the situation even more. In many cases, the police could use diplomacy and negotiation tactics to calm the suspect, so they can arrest him rather than killing him, and then he will have his day in court.

Some Ways to Improve Citizen-Police Relationships

Following are my suggestions for improving police-citizen relations:

- Additional national training guidelines might be developed for police departments throughout the nation detailing when the police should use force to protect themselves and when they should use other methods to control and subdue the suspect.
- The police might also withdraw to a safe distance when a suspect has a knife, so they are not in danger of being attacked at close quarters, which will give them more time to try to cool down the situation.
- If a suspect is running away, it is better to let that person go and seek to make an arrest later, rather than shoot that person to stop an escape.
- The participation on local citizen review boards might be expanded by including some members of the local board of supervisors in order to increase community-wide participation and facilitate more citizen and police cooperation.
- It will help to provide more transparency about police operations, such as by removing any restrictions on members of the public filming and recording the police on duty.

These measures will help the police better deal more peaceably with a current situation, while helping to build trust in the community. This approach can reduce costs, too, given the high cost of dealing with the investigation and the legal fallout following any police-citizen killing.

Police and Fatal Shootings[25]

Today, there is an apparent uptick in the number of fatal shootings of citizens by police, fanned by the media and the Black Lives Matter movement. Moreover, the perception is that the police have wantonly engaged in these killings, using racial profiling to target African Americans, who are the major victims in these shootings. Subsequently, after the officers involved have been cleared of wrongdoing as a result of administrative hearings and trials, the perception is that the criminal justice system is corrupt in letting guilty officers off because the system is wrongly protecting them. The result has been the further impression that the exoneration of these officers reflects a system-wide bias against African Americans, which has fueled further protests supporting the Black Lives Matter movement and has contributed to the growing divisiveness in U.S. society today.

However, these impressions and perceptions are misleading, because they don't take into account the difficulties which the police face. I want to examine this issue of what happens when a police officer is involved in a fatal shooting, drawing on recent research and an extensive interview with Lance LoRusso, an attorney in Georgia, who specializes in representing police officers in administrative, criminal, and civil hearings. He has written two books about fatal shootings by cops: *When Cops Kill*[26] and *Blue News*[27].

According to the National Law Enforcement Officers Memorial Fund, in 2015, 123 officers died in the line of duty, a number generally in line with previous years, and in the last four years, 40-50 officers were "shot, stabbed, strangled or beaten to death each year." So overall more police are not being killed in the line of duty, although more of those being killed may be the victims of targeted killings.

At the same time, in the number of homicides by police the U.S. Department of Justice reported 1080 deaths for 2015.[28]

LoRusso observed that the "war on the police is real," in describing some of the situations in which officers are fired upon and attacked. Ambushes are actually rare occurrences – only 21 in 2015, but they have been a key factor in increasing fear among the police and the call for more law and order by fearful citizens.

The answer isn't to reduce the police presence in communities where confrontations have occurred, since as LoRusso observed, most residents in the inner cities, where there is a high level of crime, want police protection for themselves. They don't want the police to retreat in the face of attacks by criminals and terrorists, as they have done recently in Chicago despite a real escalation of gang-related murders.

How Misinformation Leads to Anger Against Cops and the System[29]

Since the shooting of Michael Brown in Ferguson, Missouri by the police in 2014, there has been a growing anger against the police, especially after several more police shootings and other arrest incidents led to deaths. The resulting protests and riots have, in turn, triggered even more anger, much of it fueled by the media which have played up these incidents. More and more venom has been heaped on the police, who are viewed by some as out-of-control racist killers, leading to even more attacks on them and on the criminal justice system as a corrupt enabler. A common trigger for these citizen and media attacks is when police investigations lead to clearing the police officer charged with a fatal homicide.

The Major Sources of Misinformation

According to LoRusso, there are two major sources of misinformation. One occurs because citizens don't understand the police use of force guidelines, whereby the police are trained on when they can use deadly force. In addition, citizens don't understand the careful assessment of a homicide committed by a police officer, which occurs at four levels within the criminal justice system – the administrative internal review process, the criminal investigation by the police, the prosecutor's decision to charge or not charge a crime, and the courts if a trial occurs. If citizens understood this process, they would recognize that in most cases, the police officer is not at fault in using his or her gun for self-defense in these difficult confrontations. In such situations, the officer reasonably believes his or her life or that of someone else is under immediate threat and shoots for that reason.

Another source of misunderstanding is misinformation that gets out through the social media without being quickly corrected. Frequently, witnesses or activists put out false information about what actually happened to suggest that the police officer wasn't under threat, and this false information becomes the narrative that furthers hostility to the police and the system.

Misunderstandings about Use of Force

The basic policy underlying the use of force is that an officer can use deadly force when he perceives his own life or that of another party under his protection is in danger of harm from the perpetrator. Then, a further consideration is what the state statute permits, since nearly every state has a statute that justifies the use of force by law enforcement officers.

The code permits sheriffs or peace officers to use any reasonable non deadly force as necessary to apprehend and arrest a suspected felon or misdemeanant, although if the suspect resists and escalates the arrest into a confrontation where the officer fears for his life, that officer has the authority to use deadly force.

One source of misunderstanding about the use of force is what is a reasonable belief. In general, citizens don't understand that these judgments about whether the officer acted reasonably are based on what a law enforcement officer would reasonably believe is a real danger from the suspect rather than what an average citizen would believe. These beliefs can differ because the officer has a truer understanding of the nature of the danger than the average person, due to the officer experiencing many months of training on when to use deadly force in response to a perception of danger.

For example, in an interview, LoRusso pointed out how quickly a suspect can fire a gun or come at an officer with a knife, and how it can be difficult for an officer to accurately distinguish whether the suspect has a gun or not in a low light situation, which is when most citizen-police encounters occur.

Thus, in a common scenario, it might be difficult to determine whether the suspect is holding a gun which could be deadly or a cell phone which is not.

So which is it? Upon seeing the potential danger, the officer has only moments in which to react by using deadly force to protect him or herself, because if he/she hesitates and is wrong, he/she will die.

Misunderstandings about the Need for Quick Action

Generally, citizens don't understand this need for quick action, when they later claim the officer shouldn't have shot, because the suspect only had a toy gun or a cell phone. But at the time, the officer didn't know, and when the suspect didn't respond to a command to immediately put up his or her hands, the officer felt his or her life at risk. Accordingly, in such a situation, the officer is justified to shoot, though many citizens don't understand why he or she had the right to do so.

Another problem is that citizens don't understand how quickly a suspect's attack can turn deadly, which is another reason an officer might respond with deadly force rather than taking the risk that the suspect will shoot or charge with a knife.

For example, as LoRusso explained, a person with a gun in his or her belt can fire that gun in 0.2 seconds by just pointing and shooting it. Then, it takes 2.5 seconds for each follow-up shot. By contrast, he claims that if an officer tries to pull his or her gun out of his/her holster to shoot, it takes about 7.6 to 8.3 seconds, which means that if the officer waits to see if the suspect will fire, he or she will be shot and perhaps killed.

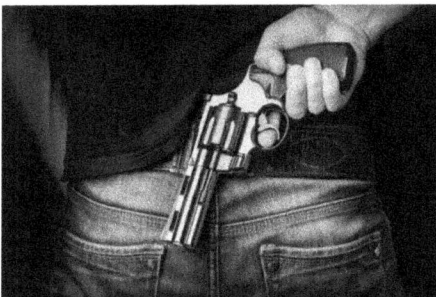

So the officer will normally already have his or her gun drawn when confronted by a potentially dangerous situation, so he or she can shoot immediately. Otherwise the person with the gun can shoot the officer three times before the officer is able to shoot back. Under the circumstances, in a low-light situation, an officer has a fraction of a second to determine whether something the suspect is holding is a weapon or a cell phone, and so is reasonably permitted to shoot to kill.

Few citizens go through a Citizen's Police Academy class where they might recognize how a delay in responding to a potentially deadly incident could be disastrous. In such a class, they experience a training simulator in which they are presented with a series of potentially deadly encounters, where the suspect has a gun, knife, or object that could be a weapon or cell phone.

Given the realities of these potentially deadly encounters, in training programs around the United States, officers are trained on how to respond quickly and intuitively, without thinking about what to do, in order to reasonably make these split second decisions. By the same token, an individual with a knife can charge an officer in a few seconds, so even if the officer sees a person threatening with a knife, that can be just as deadly if he or she doesn't already have a gun drawn and shoots first.

Unfortunately, the average citizen doesn't understand this need for the officer to respond almost instantaneously under usually low-light conditions, when a suspect is resisting and might be armed with a gun or a knife. So the citizen might readily claim an officer unjustly killed the victim and use that to fuel a protest movement to seek justice for the victim, as has occurred after numerous recent deaths by cops from Ferguson, Missouri to Baton Rouge, Louisiana. But in most of these cases, the officer was justified to shoot, as later determined through a series of hearings about the case.

The Extensive Hearings After a Fatal Shooting[30]

Citizens commonly think that the police are getting off easy after an officer shoots a citizen and is judged to not be at fault. While they attribute this result to a biased criminal justice system that is predisposed to judge the officer not guilty or not responsible, this perception is not true. As previously noted, an officer is judged based on his or her training and adherence to use of force principles, and in almost all of these shootings, the officer is judged to have followed these policies and to have only used deadly force when he or she felt a risk to him or herself or to a third party.

Not only do citizens generally not understand these policies, they do not understand the many hearings which a police officer has to undergo after such a shooting. At these hearings, the officer is judged again and again as to whether he or she followed the use of force principles and really felt that he or she or a third party was at risk of injury or death under the circumstances. Moreover, as comes out at these hearings, the citizens' original perception and beliefs about the incident are often wrong, because they are based on incorrect facts that get circulated by social media and are later reported as true by the mainstream media. But once the evidence of what actually happened is in, the officer's report about what happened becomes justified, and the false information circulating about the incident is generally refuted.

The Four Types of Hearings

As Lance LoRusso, a Georgia attorney who specializes in representing police officers involved in fatal shootings, points out, after a shooting, a police officer actually goes through four levels of hearing within the criminal justice system. These four levels of hearings include the following: an administrative internal affairs hearing, a criminal investigation by the police, a decision by the prosecutor as to whether to charge a complaint or not, and a trial if the complaint is charged.

While the officer is still at the scene of the incident, as LoRusso writes in *When Cops Kill,* he or she should "provide information to investigators to help identify a suspect who has left the scene to aid in his capture and help secure medical treatment if he is injured."[31] At this point, the officer also has to turn over his weapon and any other equipment used during the encounter.

However, immediately after the incident, the officer will often recall very little of what happened and will have difficulty answering questions or providing "coherent and complete answers," due to the stress of what happened. To ordinary citizens and activists it may appear that the officer is trying to cover up or change the narrative of what really occurred, but in fact, the officer is often in something of a state of shock and may not know what occurred. This state of shock is common when the officer is literally staring the potential for death in the face.

The Administrative Review

Almost immediately after the fatal incident, the first review is an administrative review, commonly handled by the police department's Internal Affairs Division, which looks at whether the officer correctly followed the department's use of force procedures, which were established through state law.

In some jurisdictions there also may be a citizens' review panel to look at the incident and make recommendations, usually to the police Internal Affairs Division, as to whether a crime occurred. In some cities, the review board may announce its decision publicly. While there is some controversy about the need for and propriety of such panels, the concept is firmly established in the United States. Commonly, the members of these panels include community leaders, politicians, the media, and advocates. In some communities, such as Oakland, California, which has highly antagonistic responses to the police, the review panel has a strong anti-police leaning, which has led to extensive disputes with the police union and other community members who are more supportive of the police.

The Criminal Investigation and Prosecutorial Review

The second type of review is conducted by criminal investigators from the police department. They descend on the scene, secure it, and begin processing the evidence. Commonly, they wait several days to interview the police officer who killed the suspect, because they are aware the officer is in a highly emotional shocked state. As a general rule, federal agents do not speak with anyone for at least seventy hours following a killing."[32] When this interview occurs, officers have the same rights as an ordinary citizen, in that they can ask to have an attorney present during questioning to observe the process, advise them about the questions asked and their response to them, and whether to continue the interview.[33]

Commonly, during the interview, officers will be asked to draw a diagram of the scene and indicate where they were standing, their position relative to the suspect, and how many times they fired their gun. The officer often may not recall this information and so cannot answer, because, as LoRusso points out, he or she has experienced auditory exclusion, a psychological reaction in response to intense stress that limits what a person hears.[34] Thus, though an average citizen or activist might perceive that the officer is lying or distorting what happened, actually this lack of response is due to the officer truly not recalling what happened.

If the criminal investigators find some evidence that suggests the shooting could be a crime, the third level of investigation of the fatal incident is a prosecutorial review. At this stage, the prosecutor looks at the evidence collected by the criminal investigators to determine if there is sufficient evidence to warrant a criminal trial.

Alternatively, some prosecutors may turn to a grand jury or seek to have a federal inquiry into what occurred. These grand juries are made up of individuals in the community who are selected by a court to decide if it is appropriate for the government to prosecute someone suspected of a crime. If the jurors decide that the case warrants prosecution, they will issue an indictment, after which the prosecutors will proceed. In the event that prosecutors look to the federal government for assistance, then federal prosecutors in the U.S. Department of Justice will review the case and decide if it merits prosecution. A reason that prosecutors might look to a grand jury or federal authorities is if the case has been widely publicized or has become controversial, so that opposing sides have different views as to whether a suspect is guilty or not. In this way, the prosecutor can be viewed as being more neutral in assessing the case, rather than appear to be taking sides based on popular opinion.

The Criminal Trial

Should there then be sufficient grounds for a criminal prosecution, the fourth stage is having a criminal trial, which is what happened in some high-profile cases.

For example, in Baltimore, four officers were tried when Freddie Gray suffered from injuries in the back of a police van while he was being taken to jail after an arrest. In another widely publicized case, Eric Garner died in Staten Island after an officer put him in a chokehold while he was resisting arrest. In these and many other cases, the officers were found not guilty, despite the widespread public belief that the officers were guilty and the criminal justice system was corrupt because they were set free.

However, this is where the public perception of a case can differ from the weight of the evidence and the standards of proof of intent in a criminal trial. For example, in the Freddie Gray case, a reason for the not-guilty verdict was the lack of the officers' intent in causing Gray's death, though their negligence in not securing him properly in the back of the van provided justification for a civil trial and a verdict in favor of the Gray family.

In the Garner case, a Staten Island grand jury decided not to indict any of the arresting officers involved in Gardner's death in police custody. Despite Garner's pleas that "I can't breathe" in his final moments, he was continuing to struggle, and in New York, chokeholds aren't illegal under state law when used by a cop during a lawful arrest. Even though Garner was only selling untaxed cigarettes on the street, he was committing a crime, providing a legal basis for his arrest. Unfortunately, for Garner, he was suffering from a number of medical ailments, including advanced diabetes, heart disease, and a severe case of asthma that could have easily killed him when he was subjected to what otherwise would have been an ordinary chokehold, as described in a *New York Post* article on how Garner was a victim of his own doing due to resisting arrest.[35]

The Civil Litigation

Finally, whatever the outcome of a criminal investigation or a trial, if one occurs, the officer in a fatal shooting can still be subjected to a civil lawsuit. It does not matter if the officer is found not guilty in a criminal trial, he or she still could be found responsible in a civil suit, because this has a lower burden of proof (where a preponderance of the evidence is required to find the defendant liable) than in a criminal justice hearing (where a certainty of no doubt is required to find criminal responsibility). Moreover, in the civil suit, the jurors can be swayed by outside social and media pressure, even if they are supposed to judge the evidence objectively. As a result, they may be influenced by their emotions or by popular opinion, and they may judge the officer to be at fault, despite what the evidence may show.

The High Financial and Psychological Costs

Making matters even worse for the officer is the financial burden resulting from any criminal or civil trial. While the city or county with jurisdiction over the incident may fund its own defense, the officer typically has to pay to defend him or herself. Thus, he or she faces a high risk of ruinous civil damages, and even if the officer is found not liable, he or she will still have very high expenses for a defense lawyer, since a defense can cost many thousands if not hundreds of thousands of dollars. Such a high financial hit can put the officer's home and property at risk and drain any savings. Besides having to pay for any expenses for an attorney and court costs, the officer might have to additionally pay any damages assessed if he or she loses. It is no wonder that any officer normally experiences a high level of stress, often sufficient to result in PTSD (post-traumatic stress disorder) as the officer tries to pull his or her life together after a shooting incident.

Thus, as much as many citizens may think out-of-control police officers are acting out of racial bias in shooting citizens and are protected by the criminal justice system, since they are usually found not guilty, the reality is very different. Officers generally are well aware of use of force guidelines, and they have been

48

trained to respond almost instantaneously, when they perceive a potentially deadly attack against them or a third party. They know they have to respond this way to avoid the potential death of themselves or the third party. Then, when an investigation occurs at the different levels of the criminal justice system, their response under the circumstances is carefully assessed in light of these guidelines. If they are ultimately found not guilty criminally that is because the evidence supports their response. It would seem that these four levels of adjudication provide a fair way of judging the officers, in spite of the public perception that they are being unfairly let off by the criminal justice system.

Additionally, separately from any determination by the criminal justice system, they face tremendous emotional trauma and a high level of expense. In fact, the possibility of such serious penalties for shooting a civilian could lead many officers to hold back from confronting a dangerous suspect or making an arrest, leading citizens to actually become less safe, since the criminals in such situations could escape, leaving them free to prey on other citizens again.

Still another factor making life more difficult for an officer involved in a shooting is the role of the media. Typically, the media sensationalizes the case and often sides with the victim, turning the officer into a demon in the public eye, as the following discussion of the media's role in these police killings shows.

The Role of the Media in Promoting Violence in Police Fatalities[36]

Today, both the traditional media and social media have been playing an influential role in fanning the flames of anger towards the police. To be sure, some police officers have been too quick to shoot or have improperly vented their hostility on a hapless suspect, such as the white Tulsa police officer Betty Shelby, who shot an unarmed black man, Terence Crutcher, who had his hands above his head by the side of his stalled SUV. She was later charged with a "heat-of-passion" manslaughter charge for acting unreasonably in overreacting to the incident. [37]

But in many other cases, the media simply get it wrong, and a false story is spread virally, such that many people think it is true. As a result, when the police officer is found not guilty based on the actual evidence in the case, people believe there was no justice, that somehow the fix was in, so the police officer was wrongly acquitted.

How the Media Can Spread a False Story

A classic example of spreading a false story is what happened in the case of the shooting of Michael Brown in Ferguson, Missouri by Darren Wilson, according to LoRusso. In the Brown case, what actually happened is that Brown tried to take away Wilson's gun, while Wilson was still seated in his patrol car, and the gun went off twice – one time into Brown's finger, a second time into the door. Witnesses said that Brown was running away and was shot in the back, but their narrative was later discredited by evidence from the medical examiner that showed he wasn't shot in the back.

At the time, it was already fairly dark, and no one had their cell phones out to take pictures of the incident as it occurred. Nevertheless, the false narrative went out that Brown was shot in the back while running away, and several witnesses who weren't there made claims that they saw what happened. But in fact, no one saw the whole incident, and the false narrative was spread through social media and that became the story which was picked up by the mainstream media. Meanwhile, the police delayed in releasing their own evidence-based version of the story for five days, since they were trying to vet the initial information they received. However, by then, the false narrative had gained traction, so the later release of contradictory information by the police was viewed as part of a cover-up to protect Wilson.

Unfortunately, in such cases, the media play a major role in giving legitimacy to a false story, which only furthers its spread and general acceptance. As a result, a subsequent correction several days later generally gets lost in the emphasis on the latest and breaking news in each day's news cycle – or it is viewed as a false whitewash. The media are on to the next big story, so attempts to correct the record get lost.

How the Police Should Respond to False Information

Because a story can be so distorted by public opinion and the media, LoRusso recommends that the police should get out the accurate information about a case much more quickly. A key reason for this recommendation is due to the tension between the police and media over the timeframe for releasing information to the public. The media want to put out the information immediately, while the police have traditionally sought to conduct a careful examination of the evidence to be sure whatever they report is accurate, and they want to protect their innocent until proven guilty. Since the police are unable to slow down the media, LoRusso suggests that the police must speed up releasing their information.

Additionally, LoRusso recommends that the police need to improve their relationships with the media, so they can become involved in commenting on any breaking news story much more quickly. As LoRusso writes in *Blue News,* a local story about a fatality by the police, which he calls a "critical incident," can quickly blossom into a major national or international news story that can become the narrative, even if inaccurate. As he explains:

> "Once news coverage reaches those levels, the stories seem to take on lives of their own. The news hits a twenty-four-hour news cycle...the requests for information become fluid and endless, and the resources of the law enforcement agency

become overwhelmed, often without a clear plan to handle the situation."[38]

Balancing Out What's True and False

Certainly, this spread of false stories does not mean that some more sober news articles and investigative pieces don't get it right. For example, LoRusso points out that a *U.S. News and World Report* article describes how about 99.1% of all use of force incidents are appropriate, and only about 0.9% of all complaints are cleared by imposing sanctions, which helps to put the problem of citizen deaths by police into context. Such sanctions might include suspensions or criminal charges against the officer.

However, the average citizen is not influenced as much by these actual statistics as by the sensationalized news coverage in response to individual critical incidents. This coverage plays up the violence and makes it seem that the police are at fault in most of these cases. But, in fact, the question of police fault is only raised in the very small percentage of cases that are blown up from locally covered stories into national and international news.

Then, too, this focus on certain stories makes it seem that the killings of black Americans by cops is much more common than it is, while ignoring a broader truth that most killings of blacks are due to killings by other blacks, usually by guns, as also described in my book *The Price of Justice in America*.

For example, according to LoRusso, citing a University of Toledo study on the killings by police officers between 2009 and 2012, there were a total of 56,259 homicides in the U.S., according to the Uniform Crime Reports published annually by the federal government. Out of these totals, 1491 were due to the police use of force, while 52,893 were criminal homicides or murders, which works out to about 372 persons killed by the police each year compared to about 14,065 homicides yearly. This number of 372 police homicides is also far less than the causes of other deaths –

35,900 people killed each year in motor vehicle accidents, 38,364 persons committing suicide.

That means that people are 103 times more likely to commit suicide, 97 times more likely to be killed in a vehicle crash, and 34 times more likely to be murdered by a criminal than to be killed by the police.[39]   But the media play up the individual incidents of police and citizen homicide, and the bigger picture gets lost.

The Killings of Black Males and the Police

It is also instructive to look at the relationship between the killings of black males by the police and the police killings of members of other groups to show how the media make it seem like these deaths of black males at the hands of the police are much more common than they are. For example, of the 1491 people that died from the police use of force from 2009 to 2012, 915 or 62.4% were white males, while only 481 or 32.2% were black males, and 48 or 3.2% were males of other races. Thus, the police killed more white males than black males, even though the media make it seem like there is a police vendetta against black males. Still, 32% is more than double the 13% of the population that is black.

More significantly, the statistics show that black males were much more likely to be killed by other citizens, and in particular by black males, than by the police. During this same 2009 to 2012 time period, of the 56,259 homicide during this time, 19,000 or 33.8% were killings of black males. However, only 481 or 2.5% of these killings were due to the police use of force. By contrast, substantially more – 648 or 3.4% -- were due to justified homicides by private citizens acting in self-defense, and 17,719 or 93.3% were criminal homicides by private citizens. So private citizens killed more black males than police in both justifiable and criminal homicides.

At the same time, the vast majority of these killings in both justifiable and criminal homicides were by blacks killing blacks.

While only 6% of the U.S. population is black and male, 57.9% of the individuals killed in self-defense by a private citizen were black males, and 73.1% of the black males killed under these circumstances were killed by a black citizen.

The stats also show in other ways that the major source of violence is blacks killing other blacks, rather than blacks killing or being killed by the police. For example, 90% of the black males killed in a criminal homicide were killed by another black male, whereas only 41% of the police officers killed in the line of duty were killed by black males. It is also telling that black males are 35 times more likely to be killed in a criminal homicide and equally likely to be killed in self-defense by a black citizen as they are to be killed by the police. Such statistical findings have led researchers to conclude that there is actually "significant restraint on the part of police officers nationwide in using deadly force, not an epidemic of police-initiated killings in the U.S."[40]

So why is there a false perception of widespread police killings? A key reason is the role of social media and traditional media in playing up some of the killings by the police and turning them into international stories. In turn, many activist groups, such as the Black Lives Matter movement, have played up these killings, resulting in still more media coverage. By contrast, the real story should be the high level of black on black killings, which is due, as LoRusso notes, to black involvement in a high level of violent activity. Even the Toledo study points to the "heartbreaking reality of the high suicide and violent crime rates among African American males in impoverished urban areas," a point also made in my book *The Price of Justice in America.*

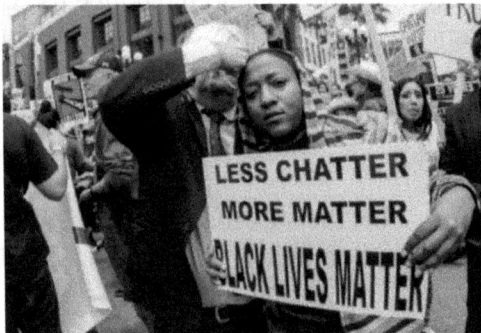

How to Correct the Misperceptions

Under the circumstances, what can be done to correct these misperceptions fanned by the media, as well as by the activists who are ready to blame the police rather than recognize the actual reality? According to LoRusso:

> "Law enforcement needs to tell the story. They should hold press conferences when there is a police fatality incident and they should give out information about any arrest in the case. They also need to correct perceptions. For example, in the Brown case, law enforcement was blamed for leaving Brown's body in the street for several hours. But in fact law enforcement is not permitted to move a body without the permission of the coroner...So law enforcement needs to quickly respond and correct any misunderstandings and misperceptions, because once bad news is out there, it stay there. Law enforcement needs to talk to the media more."

In sum, much of the misperception about the guilt of the police in most of these "use of force" fatality cases is due to the media not having the correct information in the first place and then spreading inaccurate stories that fuel hostility toward the police. These false stories result in a belief in a failure of justice, when police officers are found not guilty or innocent in most of these cases, as they should be when the evidence is viewed dispassionately by judges and jurors. Unfortunately, much of this misinformation gets spread as a result of the vacuum that often occurs in the hours or days after the incident, so false stories get out in the news. Once that happens, it becomes difficult to correct this false narrative.

Therefore, law enforcement officials have to act more quickly to get out a correct version of what really happened, and here's how they can do that more effectively. Certainly, they don't want to interfere with an investigation into the crime and the collection of evidence and testimony by witnesses. But as soon as they can, police officials need to put out the available information which they can release to the media. Or if necessary, with improved relationships with the media, these officials might be better able to get the media to publish the correct information and quickly correct or not publish inaccurate news. At the same time, the officials need to take care not to release information that might jeopardize the investigation while law enforcement is still gathering evidence of what really happened in the case.

<u>Other Police Issues</u>[41]

Now I want to discuss some additional police issues:

- Complaints of misconduct by the police
- Stop and identify laws
- Police brutality and killings
- Breakdown of law and order: killings of police and riots

Then I will provide some suggested solutions.

These issues are important since the first encounters of those who wind up in jail or prison are with police. For years blacks have complained about being profiled by police, but the past few years have been marked by an increased perception by liberals that the police are killing more and more unarmed blacks. This has sparked protests led by black lawmakers and fanned by the Black Lives Matter movement. In some instances, this perception has led to a breakdown of law and order in the form of riots and looting. Although these reactions have not been as severe as the riots in Newark, Watts or Detroit in the 1960s, a second horrendous phenomenon has appeared recently: ambush killings of police engaged in ordinary day-to-day activities. Let's consider these issues one at a time.

Complaints of Misconduct by the Police

Certain police actions might be justified under the circumstances, but they can be blown up into the police acting wrongly. An example might be where a police officer stops a motorist for what is just a routine traffic infraction. But then the citizen becomes hostile or looks like he is reaching for a gun, leading a police officer to make a split second decision to protect his or her own life. Such cases can be quickly turned into both a liberal attack on the police officer for committing murder and the police department for protecting the officer from the charge.

In such cases, it is important to look critically at the nature of the encounter to determine who is really at fault -- or if the shooting is due to uncertain actions on both sides. Such uncertainty could mean the case is more of a tragic accident based on misperception and miscommunications.

Stop and Identify Laws

The stop-and-identify laws are statutes that allow the police to detain people and ask them to identify themselves, commonly by showing an ID. If the individuals refuse to properly identify themselves or show a false ID, the police are in their rights to arrest them.

Liberals often claim that abuse occurs in those cities and states where there is a large Hispanic population, and police are using the stop-and-identify laws in order to check and see if a person is an illegal immigrant. If the person is, the police then may turn the individual over to the Immigration and Naturalization Service (INS). Under the Trump administration, this has led to confrontation between the federal government and so-called Sanctuary Cities, where local government has instructed police not to cooperate with the INS or ICE (Immigration and Customs Enforcement).

In other areas, the police might be using the stop-and-identify laws to target someone believed to be on parole or probation to investigate them further — even if the individual is not doing anything illegal at that specific point — and then find a reason to make an arrest. A scathing report was recently issued on the Ferguson, Missouri police force by the Obama administration Department of Justice for civil offenses of this sort against blacks.[42] Still, in many cases, a police officer is justified in using these stop-and-identify laws when the individual on parole or probation is in the area where a crime has just occurred and matches the description of the perpetrator.

Arrests and convictions prove particularly easy in inner city neighborhoods where drugs are openly bought and sold on the streets. One reason the police target minorities in these areas is that they are rewarded by both pay and promotions based on the numbers of arrests and convictions they make. Also, individuals in these areas, who are more likely to be involved in both selling and buying drugs, are more likely to be members of minority groups. While such arrests may be justified, often the police are more likely to make them for practical reasons. For instance, it is far easier to make arrests that lead to convictions or pleas in drug possession cases than in murder cases, which require substantially more investigative efforts.[43]

Police Brutality and Killings

Both liberals and some police officials have questioned whether the police have been too brutal in some situations. This issue has come to the fore because, as a steadfast supporter of law and order, President Trump has made statements recently condoning some aspects of police brutality as part of his stance to have police show-criminals who is boss. In response, a number of police chiefs have issued statements objecting to his attitude as counterproductive to community relations.[44]

Breakdown of Law and Order: Killings of Police and Riots

Another truly horrendous problem the police have faced recently is the killings of police in ambush attacks. This has occurred due to the growing hostility of citizens to the police in certain areas, most notably the inner cities. For example, in at least one case in Dallas, this attack may have been motivated by black anger over unarmed blacks killed by police. Such ambushes strike fear into the hearts of our police protectors and cause them to approach situations as tense as car stops with a sense that their lives are in danger. That in turn may have led to more blacks killed by police acting in fear of their lives. Thus, confrontations between police and blacks are growing ever more dangerous and need to be approached with new guidelines.

Similarly, protests by black communities over the loss of their members to police action are increasingly leading to riots and looting, which generally hurt the black communities where these incidents most often occur. In these cases, public sentiment is often revved up by the media eager to cover any confrontations live, which makes such confrontations even more likely to occur. The liberal media coverage of these confrontations has been growing ever more biased against the police since President Trump took office. Blacks and liberals have mobilized to speak out in more and more caustic, divisive terms. With each protest confrontation, the danger increases that some young African-American will want to show off by confronting the police violently.

So what can we do about this growing hostile divide between the police and citizens, especially in the black community? In the following section, I'll offer some suggestions on what to do.

Suggested Solutions[45]

We need to continue supporting our police. However, some suggestions to reduce the relatively few abuses by the police include the following:

➤ The police or a committee of legislators, possibly including some citizens should develop national training guidelines and policies for police departments nationwide. These guidelines should represent a "code of conduct" that local police departments could follow in order to improve police operations, increase compliance, and reduce citizen complaints against the police.

➤ A training program might be developed to increase police awareness of local community needs and show how officers could better interact with local citizens in a spirit of trust and cooperation.

➤ The Department of Justice could require the FBI to perform its own independent investigations of police misconduct rather than relying on information provided by the police.

➤ The media should be encouraged not to fan the waves of racial indignation with each unfortunate exceptional incident between police and blacks. This sensational news reporting may serve the media with more "Breaking News," but it does not serve the public well, and false claims of misconduct can lead to protests and even riots. The media could serve the public better with more investigative reporting regarding trends in police action and potential abuse.

➤ The police must receive additional training to help prevent racial protests from developing into race riots. That training should involve close cooperation between protest

60

organizers and the police, with the understanding that neither side nor the nation can withstand the consequences of serious race riots. Those police who provide security for protests may need to be specially selected or trained not to overreact.

Prescription: Better Safeguard our Police and Citizens[46]

We need more protections for our police because they are our first line of defense in combatting crime. The police have been demonized by many liberals and the media in America, but the overwhelming majority of police officers perform their duties selflessly and with devotion. They risk their lives every day, and their families live in constant fear that something will happen to them. They are exposed to very risk-laden situations. In spite of those dangers, surprisingly, most never use their guns or even need to draw them. But as tensions grow once more between the police and black urban communities, they need additional safeguards, and so do the citizens they apprehend.

One of the riskiest situations that police face is the normally routine car stop. Most often these stops are for minor speeding, erratic driving, or expired license plate offenses. Yet these infractions can represent just the tip of the iceberg, providing the basis for discovering much more serious offenses. In such circumstances, the driver of the car and its occupants may be very nervous and operate on a hair trigger, particularly if they have a weapon available. The outcome of these situations is all too frequently deadly, either for the driver, the police or both.

Any incident that results in the fatality of a police officer in the line of duty is a monumental tragedy that should be avoided at all costs. Any incident that results in the fatality of an innocent person represents a failure of law enforcement and most likely leads to a crushing end to the career or finances of the officer involved. Frictions between police and minority communities also need to be reduced. The following should be done to reduce the hazards of these points of police-citizen confrontation -- both to save lives and reduce costs to the criminal justice system.

> All police officers on patrol and their vehicles should be equipped with cameras that record all incidents in order to show what really happened.

> Police officers should not have to get out of their vehicle for a routine traffic stop. At night, officers should instruct drivers to turn on their car interior lights and place both hands on the steering wheel.[47] They should record the license plate of the offending vehicle and audibly advise the driver on a broadcast from their car that he or she has been issued an electronic citation which will require an appearance in court on a particular date. If and when technology permits, a photograph of a driver's license held out the driver's side window could be taken, too. These procedures to automate giving a ticket will greatly reduce the risk to police and civilians alike.

> Profiling of minorities by police should be greatly restricted to include stops only when: 1) a weapon has been displayed or fired in a local incident in the past hour, and 2) a description of *both* the suspect and a vehicle used in that incident match the vehicle spotted by the police. This requirement to connect the suspect stopped to a clear description of a wanted suspect will reduce the number of friction points between minority communities and the police and may save many innocent lives.

> Profiling minorities who are on foot in the close vicinity of a crime should be restricted to one hour following the crime. This will limit any targeting of suspects to those who can realistically be close enough to actually have committed the crime in that time frame. In the event a suspect is observed within this area in this limited time-

period, two officers must be involved in any stop and frisk apprehension. If the suspect runs, the police may follow. A single police officer should call for backup before engaging in a stop and frisk apprehension. No officer should shoot to kill unless the suspect appears to be reaching for a weapon, in which case a police officer would be justified in shooting in self-defense.

➤ The use of deadly force guidelines and the training for when to apply them need to be overhauled and standardized in order to be applied in those situations which present a clear and present danger for police officers or civilians present nearby. Currently the use of force guidelines vary widely by locality, and so does police training. While such training may be impractical for small rural police forces, their officers should be required to receive such training at the nearest larger police force facility.

PART II: PUNISHMENT AND ITS CONSEQUENCES

- **The Swamped Criminal Justice System**
- **Incarceration: Benefits and Consequences**

CHAPTER 3: THE SWAMPED CRIMINAL JUSTICE SYSTEM

We expect our criminal justice system to mete out swift justice in order to punish criminals, provide justice for their victims, and to protect society from the criminals. Unfortunately, it accomplishes none of those things expeditiously. The criminal justice system is swamped by an overload of cases due to too much crime. This has several unfortunate results.

First, justice is anything but speedy. It often takes months to schedule a court appearance after an initial arraignment.

Second, less than 5% of all cases actually go to trial. Most citizens expect a trial, preferably a trial by a jury of their peers. Very few get that. Trials are extremely time consuming and expensive. Consequently, the system has streamlined the process by having most cases decided by plea deals, almost always favoring the prosecution. It has even been mentioned that the system would collapse if all defendants insisted on trials.

Third, as a consequence of these first two factors, many of those arrested cannot afford bail and remain locked up in jail, even if they are completely innocent. Faced with the likelihood of remaining there for months and without adequate legal representation, many agree to an unwise plea deal. Those who are financially strapped do not get just treatment.

Fourth, our jails and prisons have become seriously overcrowded, necessitating the building of new ones and fostering an industry which benefits from further incarceration.

Our Criminal Justice System is a National Shame[48]

Our criminal justice system has increasingly become a national shame because it is overly costly, enmeshes too many of our citizens in the system, and may not be effective in reducing crime.

One out of every 32 Americans — approximately 7.2 million adults as of this writing — is on probation, on parole, in jail or in prison at any given time. In what has been described by liberals and the media as the prison-industrial complex, approximately 2.3 million Americans are in prison, nearly one in one hundred adults.[49] African Americans like Barack Obama and Michelle Alexander are fond of pointing out that we have 5% of the world's population, yet 25% of the world's prisoners.[50]

Our country has the highest rate of incarceration in the world — higher than Russia, China, or Iran. It is eight times higher than the rate in Germany. And it's eight times higher than we had ourselves thirty years ago.[51] We'll never be able to "Make America Great Again" if we don't fix this problem.

Who realized this was happening? Very few of us. This high rate of incarceration was all news to me. To most of us, prisons are invisible. The public is largely unaware of the prison situation, because most prisons are located in rural areas and the prison population has no voice.[52]

It's enormously expensive to incarcerate so many people. The costs of incarceration, parole, and probation in the corrections "industry" amount to over $70 billion annually.[53] This amount is as much as the food stamp program.[54] This clearly is an expensive proposition the U.S. can't afford, given a debt in the trillions. State governments are strapped and increasingly concerned with the costs of incarcerating so many. The Republican governor of my state Arkansas opted not to build a new prison and instead is sending inmates to a neighboring state, saving approximately $70 million in the process.

How did we get to this point?

Disproportionate Effects on Minority Communities

Another good reason to curtail the costly war on drugs is that a serious side effect of this war has been the unintended societal effects on minority communities. While the majority of illegal drug users and dealers throughout the U.S. are white, three-fourths of all the people incarcerated for drug offenses are African-Americans and Latinos. In 2006, one in nine 20-35 year old black men was behind bars, and far more were on probation or parole. In 2000, eight times as many whites were imprisoned for drug offenses as in 1983 (a huge increase); yet 22 times as many Latinos and 26 times as many African-Americans were imprisoned as in 1983.[3]

In some states, it's even worse:

❖ In 2000... in seven states, African-Americans constituted 80-90% of all drug offenders sent to prison.

❖ In at least 15 states, blacks are admitted to prison on drug charges at a rate 20 to 57 times greater than that of white men.[3]

The consequences of these high arrest and conviction rates are that African-American males are seven times more likely to be incarcerated than white males. As a result, one out of fifteen African-American men are in prison, compared to one out of thirty-six Hispanic men and one out of 106 white men. Disturbingly, one in three black men will spend some time in prison during the course of their lifetime.[55] That wrecks the black family structure, since it leaves the family without a provider and with young black males lacking a good male role model to help them grow up to become good citizens. This high incarceration rate for African-American males thus perpetuates crime in the black community.

The racial disparity in imprisonment results in the fact that almost half (49.4%) of incarcerated parents are black, so that African-American children are 7.5 times more likely and Hispanic children 2.5 times more likely than white children to have a parent in prison.[56] An article in the liberal *New Yorker* magazine even reported that, "In truth, there are more black men in the grip of the criminal-justice system — in prison, on probation, or on parole — than were in slavery."[57]

In turn, the effects on the economy are astronomical, given the costs involved in housing, feeding, and otherwise caring for them in prison, given the costs of imprisoning one inmate at over $30,000 a year, depending on the state.[58] And these costs are not only borne by the state or federal budget but are further vastly inflated by losses in economic productivity and family upheaval. In many instances, the incarcerated individual could instead be given a shorter sentence, released into some kind of community-based program, or required to pay restitution rather than being jailed at all.

Once branded as felons, ex-cons face legal discrimination for the rest of their lives, resulting in high costs to society as a whole. They are barred from getting food stamps and obtaining public housing for themselves and their families. Whenever they apply for a job, at most companies they have to check a box to indicate they have been in prison. They are behind the proverbial eight ball for the rest of their lives; no wonder so many fail to re-integrate into society and wind up back in prison.

Our prison policy discourages stable relationships like marriage, which is particularly fragile in the African American community. With many of the families of prisoners now living below the poverty line, U.S. welfare policy contributes to the problem by providing inadequate assistance to intact families. The AFDC (Aid to Families with Dependent Children) program unintentionally encourages African American males to stay away from the home, too.

All the way back in 1965, liberal Senator Daniel Patrick Moynihan identified the deleterious effects of this program, stating, "The steady expansion of this welfare program, as of public assistance programs in general, can be taken as a measure of the steady disintegration of the [African American] family structure."[59] This disintegration of black families can be translated into economic costs and losses to society, too, and the long-term effects on other family members result in even more negative economic consequences,

As an example of these negative consequences, both economic and social, the children of prisoners and ex-cons are increasingly troubled, and more likely to suffer from mental illness. They are likely to be poor, homeless, academically-challenged, and physically aggressive. Often they end up in prison themselves, continuing the vicious cycle.[60] Impoverished urban black ghettos are cauldrons for crime – both because crime contributes to these impoverished conditions and these conditions lead to crime.

Something, obviously, is awry in America — one of the most developed countries in the world! Why do we have such a high rate of incarceration in our nation? What are the staggering costs to society?[61] And what can we do about it?

Powerful Prosecutors Misbehaving[62]

Prosecutors wield extraordinary power, but just as easily as they can put true criminals behind bars, they can destroy the lives of innocent defendants. Prosecutors are expected to seek truth and justice, and it is important to support prosecutors who are dedicated to those goals. After all, they are part of our defense against the bad guys.

But prosecutors are also saddled with tremendous pressure from supervisors to aggressively pursue convictions or score "winning" plea bargains. Often the push to gain convictions — and the praise that follows a conviction — can overcome the prosecutorial directive to seek what is true and just. So prosecutors selectively choose which cases to prosecute and how, with limited checks on their conduct. As a result, due to prosecuting individuals who may be innocent or bringing too many charges in a case, prosecutors can end up with more convictions and more in prison who shouldn't be there or who are subjected to inordinately long sentences.

In fact, a recent 2017 book by John Pfaff even concluded that prosecutors are the single group most responsible for our bloated prison system. This is on account of their successful convictions of low-level criminals involved in non-violent crimes who received harsh prison sentences. Additionally, in many cases they have obtained convictions against defendants who were later found not guilty.[63]

Although more than 700 prosecutors in California committed prosecutorial misconduct between 1997 and 2009, according to state, federal, and appellate court opinions, a Santa Clara University School of Law study noted that the authorities failed to either report or even discipline these prosecutors. The California State Bar disciplined only six of the prosecutors involved.[64]

The charges against prosecutors get even worse. In a series of lengthy article on prosecutorial misconduct, journalists Ken Armstrong and Maurice Possley of the *Chicago Tribune* reported, "With impunity, prosecutors across the country have violated their oaths and the law, committing the worst kinds of deception in the most serious of cases... They do it to win. They do it because they won't get punished."[65]

> "The U.S. Supreme Court declared that misconduct by prosecutors is so reprehensible that it warrants criminal charges and disbarment.[59] But not one of those prosecutors who was charged with misconduct was convicted of a crime. Not one was barred from practicing law. Instead, many saw their careers advance, later to become judges or district attorneys."[59]

There is no indication the situation has improved since that time. Many of the now-publicized cases of prosecutorial misconduct in convictions incorrectly used DNA evidence to support their cases. Because of this behavior, more than 250 defendants who were convicted of crimes they did not commit have been exonerated — a revelation exposed only as a result of appeals. Barry Scheck of the Innocence Project notes that only a small number of prosecutors have been sanctioned (punished or reprimanded), even when acts of misconduct have led to cases being overturned. As he observed:

> "Our system rarely disciplines, much less brings criminal charges against prosecutors who have engaged in acts of intentional misconduct. Far too often, prosecutors, who wield enormous power over our lives, aren't investigated at all, even for intentional misconduct that has led to a wrongful conviction, much less 'harmless' intentional misconduct in cases in which the defendant was guilty."[66]

Major Types of Prosecutorial Misconduct

One of the most common types of prosecutorial misconduct is not providing the defense team with all the evidence the prosecution has gathered, in particular evidence that is exculpatory (favorable to the defendant). While prosecutors are constitutionally obligated to share any evidence favorable to the defendant with the defense, they are essentially immune from prosecution themselves. Consequently, prosecutors often ignore this obligation.

While the outcome of a wrongly convicted defendant may be shocking due to the injustice caused by a vengeful or neglectful prosecutor, another result is higher economic costs due to a wrongful incarceration. Not only are there costs of maintaining the convict in prison, but there is the loss of income from a productive citizen. Later lawsuits from defense attorneys may result, too, due to wrongful conviction and imprisonment. Worst of all, the actual perpetrator of the crime may still be at large and committing further crimes.

One high-profile case where the prosecutors concealed evidence to win a case against a high-profile defendant is that of Senator Ted Stevens, a Republican seeking re-election in Alaska. The case revolved around a charge that Stevens had failed to report more than $250,000 in illegal gifts and home renovations received between May 1999 and August 2007. The defendant insisted that he had intended to pay for all of the work performed on his house.

The jury found Stevens guilty of seven felony counts for failing to disclose the renovations and other gifts. A few days after this verdict, Stevens, the longest-serving Republican Senator in history, narrowly lost his re-election bid.

But he wasn't actually guilty and didn't need to drop out or lose the election. Less than a year later, a U.S. District Judge threw out the case at the request of the Justice Department, which found that exculpatory evidence had been withheld at the trial. Thus, since the prosecutors had won their conviction through intentionally withholding and concealing evidence, the guilty verdict was overturned.

The prosecutors in question escaped with little punishment aside from an admonition for their bad behavior. And, of course, taxpayers had to foot the bill for what turned out to be a wrongly pursued prosecution. Plus, of course, Stevens lost the election, which he was otherwise likely to win. This deprived his constituents of his service, as well as throwing his life into unnecessary turmoil and expense.

Sometimes prosecutors deliberately reveal prejudicial and inflammatory information to the press to support their personal belief that a defendant is guilty in advance of a trial. This is exactly what a prosecutor did in the notorious Duke University lacrosse team case in which three players were falsely accused of rape. The prosecutorial misconduct was so great in this case that the prosecutor, Mike Nifong, was criminally charged for his crime, disbarred, fined, convicted, and served a short jail sentence. The sanctions put on Nifong were truly exceptional; it is extremely rare that prosecutorial misconduct is punished.

So if politics was Nifong's motivation, are there other reasons for prosecutorial misconduct? Why is prosecutorial misconduct so rampant? And what can be done about it, because this not only results in false convictions and imprisonment, but high costs borne by the courts and correctional system. If the defendant is convicted, there are also losses to the economy and destabilization of the convict's family, since he is removed from the local community while in prison.

Suggested Solutions[67]

> ➢ Just as lawyers need to go back every year or two for refresher classes on ethics, prosecutors should be required to attend a similar program for prosecutors each year to remind them of their sworn duty to pursue the truth.

> ➢ We must address the real need for qualified (restricted), as opposed to absolute, immunity for prosecutors.

An Example of a Successful Solution in Action

Here's an example of a successful solution which occurred when a prosecutor sought the truth, rather than expedient resolution of cases.

The success occurred when Texas's Dallas County elected a new District Attorney, Craig Watkins, in 2006. The first-ever African-American elected district attorney in Texas history, Watkins took a very different stance toward criminal prosecutions than his predecessors.

Since Dallas had a questionable record in having more DNA exonerations than any other county in the U.S., Watkins partnered with the Innocence Project of Texas to review hundreds of requests for DNA testing. This partnership gained national attention. In addition, Watkins made other fundamental local changes that affected far more cases by shaking up his office. To do so, he first framed and placed on walls through the office an article of the Texas Code of Criminal Procedure with this one sentence highlighted: "It shall be the duty of all prosecuting attorneys, including any special prosecutors, not to convict but to see that justice is done." Then, he fired some top-level prosecutors, because they did not adhere to this code. Others left.[68]

Watkins also was guided by the policy expressed in this quotation: "Our success is not going to be based on the number of folks we send to prison or death row. That's just evidence of the failure of the criminal justice system."[69]

In turn, Watkins was praised for his actions by Texas lawyers, such as Mark Donald, who had this to say:

"...(Watkins) delicately balances the traditional role of a prosecutor as community enforcer against the more holistic approach of a prosecutor as community problem-solver. That balance has Watkins one day issuing a press release announcing he will seek the death penalty against an alleged cop killer and the next day rewarding a prosecutor for initiating a Big Brother program that pairs DA staffers with the children of inmates. It has him one day touting his new absconder unit, which will hunt down the most violent probation violators before they can victimize again, and another day selling his ideas about a community court system so neighborhood elders can punish defendants in such a way that victims will be made whole again."[69]

In response to these policies committed to upholding true justice, voters re-elected Watkins in 2010. Kudos to Watkins—and kudos to those Texas citizens.

The Media Make Matters Worse[69]

Today, the media have become complicit in producing unfair treatment, trials, and verdicts for defendants. They sensationalize cases, pick and choose whatever elements of a case make it unusual and "newsworthy," and otherwise draw what often becomes negative public attention to private citizens.

Suggested Solutions[70]

➤ Names of individuals charged with a crime should not be reported by the media. Reports should mention only that individuals have been apprehended and whether or not they were released on bail. This anonymity should also remain in the case during and after a trial, unless the trial results in a guilty verdict.

➤ The media should not be allowed to report what they learn from prosecutors, unless the defense lawyers are also allowed to comment on that information.

➤ The standard for a reporter or publication should be changed from reporting what is simply alleged or rumored to reporting what is actually known or making it very clear that there is a lack of actual facts in a case. Reporters should not be allowed to use the term "alleged" to permit the attribution of false and damaging claims to an individual or organization.

CHAPTER 4: INCARCERATION: BENEFITS AND CONSEQUENCES

How Did We Get Here?[71]

Recent History of Incarceration in the U.S.

As indicated on the graph below,[72] a greater than 5-fold rise in incarceration began in state prisons in the 1970s and continued until about 2008 through both three Republican and two Democratic Presidencies. Many people are also held in local jails, sometimes for months or even years before their trial or sentencing.

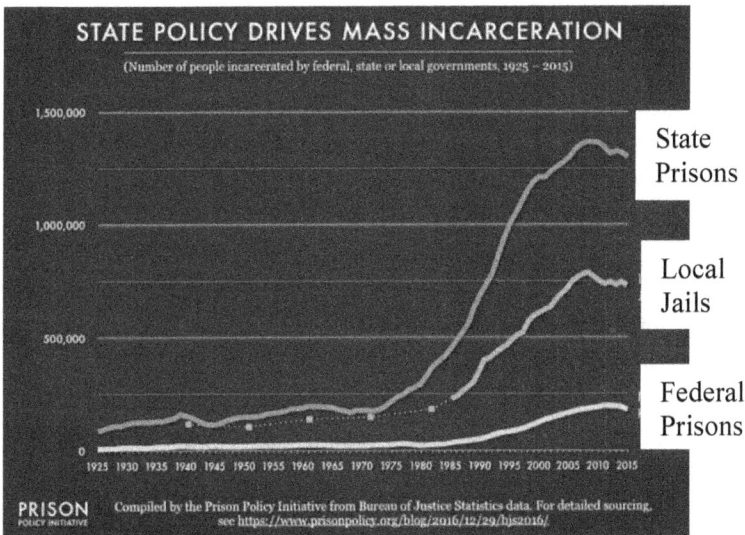

STATE POLICY DRIVES MASS INCARCERATION

(Number of people incarcerated by federal, state or local governments, 1925 – 2015)

State Prisons
Local Jails
Federal Prisons

PRISON
POLICY INITIATIVE   Compiled by the Prison Policy Initiative from Bureau of Justice Statistics data. For detailed sourcing, see https://www.prisonpolicy.org/blog/2016/12/29/hjs2016/

After 2008, incarceration plateaued at all levels -- local, state, and federal, and even showed signs of a slight decrease.

Causes for the Rise in Incarceration

Successive administrations from John F. Kennedy on to George H. W. Bush recognized the problem of crime in urban black ghettos, but they were unable to stop its growth with either liberal or conservative tactics. Both liberal and conservative administrations increased incarceration in response to concern among whites that crime would spread to their communities. The great riots in Watts in Los Angeles in 1965 and in Newark and Detroit in 1967 changed that concern about crime to real fear, and law and order became the cry among politicians of both stripes. Even as far back as the late 1970s, FBI data suggested that only about 250,000 criminals pursue careers in street crime.[73] Yet, now that we're incarcerating nearly ten times that many prisoners, we still have more crime than we did then.

The many alternate liberal strategies to solving the crime problem have not worked, after being tried unsuccessfully over 50 years ago, when the crime problem was much less acute than it has become. These efforts have included more community policing, police urban outreach programs, attempts to improve the conditions and security in substandard public housing projects, and increased job training. But none of these approaches have worked, primarily because of insufficient job opportunities for black ghetto dwellers.[74] Greater incarceration became the only alternative.[75] As Richard Nixon explained in his call for a crackdown in crime in 1968: "Doubling the conviction rate in this country would do more to cure crime in America than quadrupling the funds for …(the) war on poverty."[76]

One result of this strategy was a massive drop in the income level of black households, as a result of the increasingly vast number of African-American males being carted off to prison for longer and longer terms. Or to put this conclusion more starkly in numbers, by 2000 the net financial assets of the top fifth of all black households ($7448) was only $448 higher than the lowest fifth of white households.[77]

Greater incarceration reflected the growing public attitude towards what Peter Enns called "public punitiveness." He came to this conclusion after conducting a more detailed analysis of the causes of the increased incarceration. To conduct his study, Peter Enns assessed public opinion about crime after World War II in response to various surveys that he condensed into a factor he termed public punitiveness.[78] He argued convincingly that the root cause of the increase in incarceration was this public punitiveness driven by the media, whereby the public demanded more law and order. This demand drove politicians of all stripes to enact the policies that resulted in increased incarceration.

To a great extent this growth of incarceration was due to a response to an urban crime wave in the 1960s, but then that led to an overreaction that has simply upped costs, for more police, more courts and more prisons. This response to a crime wave is well documented in Barry Latzer's book *The Rise and Fall of Violent Crime in America.*[79] Latzer suggests that the migration of blacks from the rural South to northern cities after World War II was the key factor initially, since the homicide rate of blacks at the time was 10 times that of whites. As a consequence, a new wave of violent crime began in the 1960s in the larger cities, where most of the victims as well as most of the perpetrators were black. This high urban crime rate may well have been due to the low economic status of both victims and perpetrators there.

In addition to the black urban migration, Latzer suggests that more baby boomers reaching adolescence contributed to the crime wave, because they overwhelmed the resources of the criminal justice system.[80] The response of the system was to increase incarceration. According to Latzer, the crime wave abated in the 1990s as a result of a combination of more police, more effective policing, increased commitments to prison, and increases in time served for violent crimes.

An Analysis of Violent Crime and Incarceration Statistics Since 1960

This analysis of violent crime and incarceration statistics[81] since 1960 shows the following major patterns:

- ❖ The rise in violent crime preceded and drove the initial rise in incarceration up until 1992;

- ❖ Incarceration continued to rise after 1992, finally causing violent crime to fall;

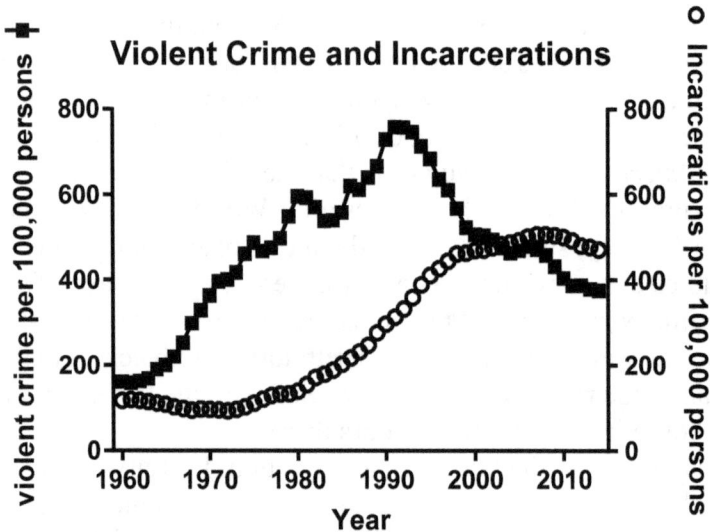

Violent Crime and Incarcerations

Note that violent crime rates peaked in 1992 and then declined. However, incarceration rates continued to rise until 2007. Thus, there was an approximately 15-year period when crime was falling and incarceration rising. After 2002 incarcerations actually surpassed violent crime. This data leads to the following conclusions:

First, over the period 1974 to 1992, when violent crime and incarceration were both increasing, incarceration rates were driven by violent crime rates.

From 1993 to 2005, increased incarceration caused a decrease in violent crime:[82]

Since 2006, both crime and incarcerations declined, suggesting that a decrease in violent crime is driving the decrease in incarcerations.

The Mechanisms Used to Increase Incarceration

❖ harsher sentencing laws, including mandatory minimum sentencing for many crimes;

❖ three-strikes and you're out laws, whereby even a minor third felony conviction resulted in an extremely long sentence;

❖ harsh sentencing for non-violent drug possession or dealing of even small amounts of drugs.

However, while these are recognized as contributing causes, an even greater role was and still is played by prosecutors, accord to John Pfaff's 2017 book *Locked In*. As Pfaff points out, prison admissions per prosecutor rose from 9 in 1974 to 25 in 1990 and essentially stayed at similar levels since then.[83] Between 1994 and 2008, the rate at which prosecutors filed felony charges rose almost 40%.

Prosecutors are able to exert so much influence because they have a great deal of power. Unfortunately, as mentioned previously, they often abuse that power.

Summing Up

This analysis has led to the following conclusions:

❖ Media coverage of anarchy starting in the 1960s stoked public fears about violent crime and fueled a demand for law and order.

❖ Politicians from both parties were fearful of seeming too soft on crime, so they pushed through punitive measures designed to lock up as many criminals as possible.

❖ Violent crime has diminished since its peak in the 1990s.

❖ Incarceration may have helped reduce violent crime in the 1990s, but it has not further reduced crime for at least 15 years.

Facts about Our Prisons and Correctional System[84]

The number of prisoners incarcerated isn't the only factor driving up prison costs. Just like the rest of the criminal justice system, prison costs are skyrocketing because of a number of factors, as described in the next section on the prison system today.

The Cost of Prisons

Today, the cost of prisons and the rest of our correctional system are out of control. We are spending far more than we need to, and we are getting poor results. Let me explain.

We spend $260 billion annually on criminal justice, $60-70 billion on prisons and jails alone. Most prisons are run by the states, not by the federal government. If all of them were federal prisons, the $60 billion it takes to run them would seem relatively modest in comparison to the defense budget, Social Security and Medicare, each of which are more than 10 times higher. The costs to individual states and localities are significantly higher in proportion to their budgets, since states spend up to 3% of their budgets on prisons and counties spend roughly 2% of their budgets for jails.[85] However, many politicians are less concerned by the high cost of incarcerating people than they are by the great public concern about crime. Public concern has been fanned by the media since the 1960s and is an even greater concern to politicians anxious to be re-elected than is fiscal prudence.

The Prison System

While liberals tend to make a big stink about private prisons, currently our prison system is overwhelmingly a public prison system. At present, most prisoners (1,330,000) are housed in state prisons rather than federal ones, which house only 197,000 inmates.[86]

Nearly all our prisons emphasize the punishment of offenders and provide a very abusive and degrading environment, both in the way inmates are treated by corrections officer staff and by fellow prisoners. Staff are often paid low salaries, experience bad encounters with inmates, and exhibit high turnover, 20-30% annually.[87]

Some prisons are also severely overcrowded and house prisoners together. Many in hot climates are not air conditioned.

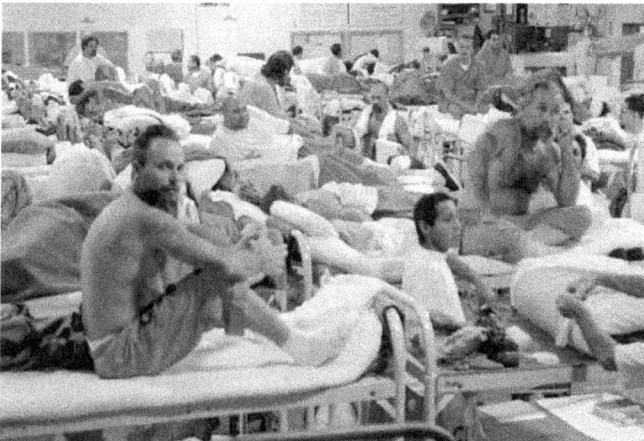

One harsh reality of prisons is that they contribute to racial conflict, not just between prisoners, but also with prison guards, the majority of whom are white due to the rural location of many prisons. Most of these guards know no blacks other than prisoners, which reinforces their feelings of superiority. In turn, their attitude probably contributes to the harsher disciplinary treatment black prisoners receive.

A second harsh reality is that prisons generate what prisoners consider a form of slave labor, where inmates work in "correctional industries" doing things like preparing license plates for wages that amount to an average of less than $3.50 a day, far below any minimum wage.

It is reasonable that a good proportion of the money the prisoners earn should be taken by the prison system for food and lodging. However, prisoners would be less resentful of the practice if they were allowed to keep more of their pay. This extra pay could then be kept in savings accounts that the prisoners can only access upon their release. The advantage of holding onto these funds is that they would make a significant difference in helping the prisoners successfully re-enter society.[88]

Solitary Confinement

Solitary confinement is another overused penalty in prison that adds unnecessary costs, too. Approximately 80,000 incarcerated individuals are held in solitary confinement, in individual cells by themselves 23 hours a day. They are allowed only one hour outside their cells for exercise and showers perhaps twice a week.[89]

Solitary confinement of this sort drives men mad. It is utilized too frequently as an unnecessary and counterproductive form of punishment. It needs to be reserved as a last resort for inmates who are a serious risk to other inmates or prison staff.

Federal Prisons

Former NYPD Commissioner, lifelong law and order Republican, Bernard Kerik severely criticized the low security federal prisons for housing the first time and seasoned criminals together. It is, as he describes it, "a school for convicts."[90] It seems likely that this situation may occur in other prisons or jails, and should be further researched.

Private Prisons

Private for-profit prisons have flourished in an environment where insufficient prison beds were available due to the high number of both state and federal prisoners.

A big problem is that for-profit private prisons are flawed by their business model. They can become more profitable if they provide the prisoners with less.[91] In addition, their business model is based on a continuous desire to expand, but they can only do so if mass incarceration is increased, which is in the interests of private prison corporation shareholders but not in the interests of the country. Liberal fears about private prisons are overblown, however, because only 8% of the prison population is housed in private prisons.

The Prison-Industrial Complex

The prison-industrial complex is another source of extra costs, due to private contracts that provide opportunities for excess payments. This is the case because private companies own contracts for generating many prison products and for providing many prison services. Those companies negotiate contracts with the prisons to provide items like license plates at very low cost because the prisoners are paid next to nothing at all. So prisoners are kept in a state of near slavery, making it more difficult for them to have the funds needed to support themselves after being released. Consequently, they are less able to become productive citizens and more likely to return to crime.

Additionally, private companies are allowed to charge outrageous rates for telephone calls between inmates and families and for all necessary personal hygiene and other items inmates must buy at the prison. The companies which provide food to prisons maximize their profits by providing the cheapest, and possibly least nutritious, food possible. The companies stocking commissaries and providing other services to prisoners likewise rake in the profits at inmates' and inmate families' expense.

Local Jails

The high jail population includes many defendants who have not been convicted, but are simply waiting for their case to be adjudicated because they cannot afford bail. Here's a breakdown of the extent of the problem.

We have a staggering 11.6 million jail admissions each year![92] One reason this number is so high is that jail stays tend to be much shorter than prison stays, since the jail population consists of either defendants awaiting trial or convicts who are sentenced for up to one year for misdemeanor and felony verdicts. The jail population at any one moment in time is considerably lower than the prison population, but still significant

Of the total admissions at any given time, local county jails house approximately 630,000 people, of which only 187,000 have been convicted. The remaining 443,000 arrestees[93] are held in these county jails for indeterminate times, because they fail to meet bail and because the justice system is so backed up that it takes weeks for a defendant to go to trial or even have his attorney work out and agree to a plea deal.

The Parole and Probation Systems

While parole and probation can be a way to reduce costs through transferring many prisoners from prisons, they are often not up to the task because of their own limitations, primarily due to insufficient funding and staffing. Here's what's wrong with these systems and how they can be fixed.

Because both the parole and probation systems are understaffed, the caseloads for both parole and probation officers are well above those that are recommended.[94,95,96] This understaffing means that felons are not adequately enough supervised to prevent them from committing new crimes -- which can be very costly. Second, understaffing results in caseworker stress and burnout, which adds costs due to the need to train new caseworkers because of the very high rates of turnover, 20-30% nationally.[97]

Such high turnover has the consequence that new caseworkers, usually inexperienced, have to supervise the parolees. For parolees, this is a clear disadvantage, because the continuity of their supervision is disrupted, with negative results. Frequently, they have to start over from scratch with their new parole officer, which can be very destabilizing for their reintegration back into the community. As a result, they may be more likely to reconnect with their old buddies with criminal records and return to crime.

Parole

The parole system is designed to take effect after time in prison, and it currently keeps 840,000 felons[98] under the supervision of 11,000 parole officers[99] attached to courts around the U.S.

Done well, parole can reduce recidivism. However, when the system is overloaded because it doesn't have enough caseworkers, it will save a state some money compared to keeping a convict in prison, but it won't reduce recidivism (repeat offenses by ex-cons). An overloaded parole system fails to reduce recidivism because a caseworker with too many cases to handle is unable to provide the necessary supervision to help an ex-con avoid turning back to crime. Thus, inadequate supervision eventually leads back to prison for many ex-cons.

The 11,000 parole officers nationally would at most be able to handle 440,000 of the 840,000 felons.[98]

In some states there are even policies that turn parole officers into financial collection agents. This compromises their ability to effectively supervise parolees. For example, in Arkansas, parole officers are also required to collect 80% of supervision fees from parolees.[100] This puts great pressure on both parolees, who may be penniless, and parole officers. These charges could actually lead parolees to commit crimes to get the funds to pay for their supervision -- an example of the system undermining its own purpose.

Probation

The probation department similarly suffers from too many cases per officer and mismanagement. The probation system exists in parallel with the prison system and it is designed for individuals who are convicted of less serious offenses. Instead of going to prison or jail, convicts are sentenced to serve their time outside of prison or jail but under probation. Besides providing less severe punishment for lesser crimes, the system was designed to relieve pressure on the overcrowded prison and jail systems.

There are far more people on probation (3,700,000)[101] than on parole, in prison or in jail, and they are supervised by only 60,000 probation officers.[102] Unfortunately, the caseload for probation officers may also be too high to keep recidivism down: a study in Iowa found a 47% decrease in recidivism for property or violent crime when probation officer caseload was reduced 40%.[103] However, these caseloads have not been reduced more generally.

Putting convicts on probation rather than sending them to jail is more cost-effective, and any programs to reduce the caseload of probation officers would contribute significantly to reducing recidivism and therefore the costs of crime.

Different Types of Prisoners

Prisoners over 50 substantially drive up healthcare costs to prisons, and they are far less likely to commit crimes. It would be well worthwhile to consider early parole for older prisoners, particularly if they have a family or other support structure available to them on the outside.

The mentally ill and addicted represent another category of prisoners which abound in prisons. The population of the mentally ill in state mental institutions plummeted from 560,000 in 1955 to 160,000 in 1976,[104] and prisons have become the repositories for the mentally ill. The prisons are ill-equipped to deal with them. Ten times as many mentally ill are incarcerated in prison as in state hospitals.[105]

Representative Tim Murphy (R-Pa) claims that the majority of those in state and local jails have a mental disorder.[106] This shocking claim is borne out by statistics, as seen in the following table, with the possible exception of those in federal prisons. The percentage of male and female inmates with at least one mental health problem in different kinds of institutions is shown in the table below.[107]

	Male inmates with at least one mental health problem	Female inmates with at least one mental health problem
State prisons	55%	73%
Federal prisons	44%	61%
Local jails	63%	75%

Former NYPD Commissioner Bernard Kerik states: "People who need treatment for drug or mental health problems do not belong in prison. They belong in treatment centers."[108]

Prisoners with learning or cognitive disabilities also fill up the prisons because they lack the skills needed to get a job. Because of these disabilities, many prisoners had to repeat grades and became high school dropouts at higher risk for incarceration. Learning/cognitive disabilities include dyslexia[109] (making reading extremely difficult) and attention deficit hyperactivity disorder (ADHD).[110]

Compared to ADHD, prisoners are even more likely to suffer from dyslexia, whereby one mixes up the order of letters and therefore has trouble reading and learning. According to recent research, approximately 5-17% of the population have dyslexia. This condition, if untreated, can, in turn, lead to crime and is common in prison and jail inmates. About 2 in 10 prisoners have a cognitive disability, as do 3 in 10 jail inmates (several times that of the general population).[111]

Gang members represent another category of problem prisoners. Gang violence occurs in the prisons, and gang leaders in prison direct those outside to engage in gang violence against opposing gang members as well as participate in organized criminal activity. In effect, criminal activity increased by incarceration has become an alternate form of business enterprise in lieu of other meaningful opportunities for financial success. In this way, gang leaders not only engage in criminal activity within the prison, but they use their prison connections to participate in an alternate form of business activity. Then, when released, they continue in this business activity if they don't have other meaningful opportunities for making money.

These observations about forms of incarceration, parole, probation, and the many types of problem prisoners lead to the following conclusions.

<u>Summing Up</u>[112]

- ❖ **observations**
- ➢ **recommendations**

- ❖ This high rate of incarceration costs far too much financially and in terms of our international image.

- ❖ Too many of those in jails have not been convicted.

  - ➢ Probation and parole are ways to reduce the prison population for those who have committed less serious crimes, and costs are much less than for imprisonment.

  - ➢ Since caseworkers are overwhelmed with too many cases to supervise them adequately, reduce caseworker caseloads by reducing sentences for prisoners with less serious crimes, by moving the mentally ill to other facilities, and by hiring more caseworkers.

Move the Ill and Mentally Ill to Other Facilities

- ❖ Too many of those incarcerated are elderly with costly health problems.

- ❖ Too many of those incarcerated are mentally ill.

  - ➢ The mentally ill could be better served in other facilities that could provide them with better treatment at a lower cost.

Reduce the Number of Prisoners with Problems of Substance Abuse or Learning Disabilities

- ❖ Too many of those incarcerated have substance abuse problems requiring treatment, but they generally don't receive it. They emerge from prison with substance abuse problems that increase their chances of being arrested and winding up back in prison.

More recommendations will follow in Part III, and still others may be found in my book *The Costly U.S. Prison System*.

Families Suffer Collateral Damage Due to the High Incarceration Rate[113]

By way of introduction to this topic, I have recently been paying attention to the media coverage of crime and have become aware of how really distorted the information we get from the media truly is. A case in point is the lack of stories about families in trouble due to incarceration of a loved one. Instead, the big story is about the crime, the conviction, and the killer.

The problem is that the media plays up the drama of police arrests and convictions, and once a defendant or victim is well-known, their story is what is featured in the news. Likewise, the protests that erupt over especially controversial police actions receive a lot of media attention, particularly when these protests might turn violent.

The Forgotten Families

Forgotten in this media and public attention are the families of the victims or the convicted and incarcerated defendant. The justice system offers only some sympathy to victims' families, and certainly none to defendants' families, though family stability and values provide the backbone for a strong society. These families are the forgotten casualties of the criminal justice system.

In my view, these family victims represent "collateral damage." It's a term commonly used to refer to the unintended damages from a military operation, which includes the destruction of civilians. This term fits the family of a prisoner, too, because whenever a family member is incarcerated or killed, there can be great damage to family units – including spouses, children, parents, and relatives, and all of the defendant's or victim's relationships. Stories of murders generally focus on the investigation and defendants, who are impacted negatively at all stages of a prosecution, from the initial charge to the trial and verdict. But what happens to their family members is largely ignored by the media and public.

Unfortunately, these damages can be huge and lifelong. When a male who has been the major family provider is killed or sent to prison, the family may become financially unstable. The wife may not make enough with a single income to pay the bills, and other relatives and friends may not be in a position to help. So after a few months or perhaps a year, the family may end up losing its home or be unable to pay the rent and end up living in a car, van, or truck, or worse – reduced to living in a tent.

Some of the cities with a high homeless population, such as San Francisco and Oakland, have found that a large percentage – about a quarter to a third of the homeless population – was formerly part of the middle or working class and until recently had homes. But then, due to an unlucky break, such as having a main provider incarcerated or the victim of a crime, they ended up as a homeless statistic.

Moreover, the children may suffer lasting damage, finding it difficult to cope with a parent's incarceration or death due to a violent crime.

Reducing the Collateral Damage

What is the solution to help reduce the collateral damage? One approach is to provide extra counseling, tutoring and mentoring support through the schools to the children of incarcerated parents. Support programs could be established for the wives and children of returning prisoners, much like for the families of returning soldiers to help them better know and adjust to the difficulties ahead. Also, the partners of prisoners could form small support groups to take care of each other's children when at work or during prison visits. Additionally, I recommend the expansion of re-entry and job training for prisoners and ex-prisoners to help them successfully enter normal society. All of these programs can be provided at a low cost to reduce the collateral damage problem, while helping the families become more productive members of society. In my view, these approaches can be a win-win for both the prisoners and their families and for society as a whole.

How many families are affected? We'll see below.

The World Leader in Incarcerations[114]

Though most U.S. citizens are probably unaware of this, the U.S. leads the world in incarcerations.[115]

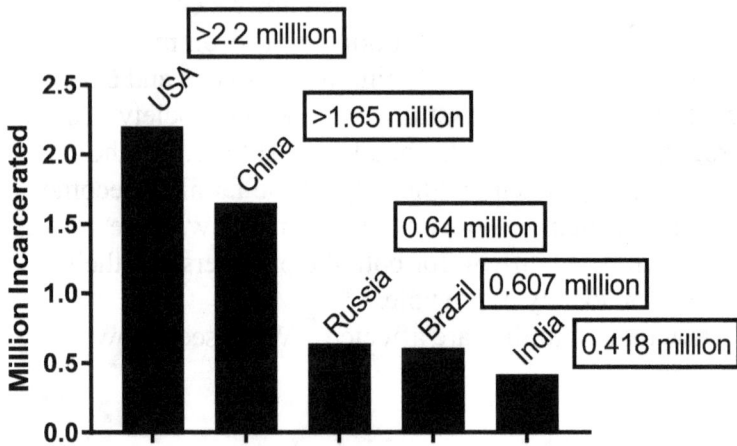

Top 5 Countries for Incarceration

If you normalize (divide) by the population for each country, the U.S. still tops the list.[3]

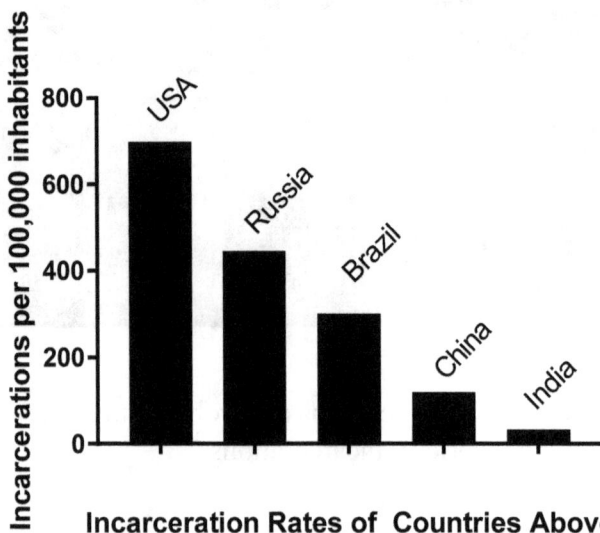

Incarceration Rates of Countries Above

For a country that prides itself on its human rights record and seriously criticizes countries like Russia and China for their poor treatment of people, we should examine-ourselves closely to make sure we are not guilty of hypocrisy. We could be accused of having our own gulag, given our horrendous incarceration record.

Why Do We Have So Many Prisoners?

Many people believe the myth that we have so many more prisoners because we are a much more violent nation than others. This isn't the case.

Russia and Brazil have a much higher murder rate than we do.[116] Therefore, there is no real excuse for the vast number of prisoners we have incarcerated. We have imprisoned so many millions in response to a crime wave that began in the 1960s. That may have helped reduce crime levels, but we still haven't fixed the crime problem sufficiently, and we have now added the additional problem that incarceration compounds the social ill that plagues our cities. That's because this extensive incarceration has further eroded the social structure of impoverished urban black communities, and this deterioration of the social structure of poor communities will continue to foster crime for decades to come unless we treat the condition that leads to criminal behavior -- much of it the result of poverty in the inner cities.

Ironically, we Americans pride ourselves on being first in many things, but incarceration should not be one of those. We experience similar levels of crime as European countries, but more violent crime,[117] and victims are more likely to die in the U.S. It is likely that the fear of violent crime has led us to demand tougher punishment.[118] The result is on average about a six times higher incarceration rate than Europe has.

Now let's consider parole and probation. Many other countries don't have parole or probation systems. The difference between the U.S. and other countries is even more extreme than the differences in the charts on page 100, if you add in those on parole and probation.[119]

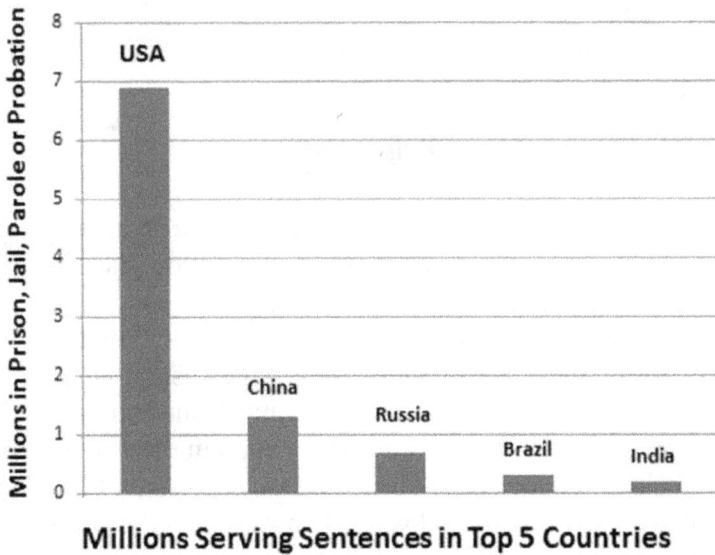

Millions Serving Sentences in Top 5 Countries

As the chart above shows, the U.S. has nearly 7 million people incarcerated, on parole or on probation compared to well under 1.5 million in China, and less than a million in any other country. In fact, over half of those in correction in the world are serving sentences in the U.S. This horrific situation does have at least one very slim silver lining for an offender and another for taxpayers. For offenders, it is better to be on parole or probation, since these offer more freedom than being confined in a prison or jail cell. For taxpayers, the cost of supervision on parole or probation is considerably less than the cost of prison or jail. However, despite these savings, we skimp too much on parole and probation supervision. As a result, the parole and probation systems are both understaffed.

This understaffing causes problems because it contributes to the increase in crime by those on probation or parole and don't get the supervision and support they need to re-integrate into society (those on parole) or keep to the straight and narrow (those on probation) and become productive citizens.

The Worst Investment in the U.S.[120]

More prisons may be the worst investment this country can make. Former Supreme Court Justices Stephen Breyer and Anthony Kennedy denounced the criminal justice system to a Congressional subcommittee in 2015, noting that it costs approximately $30,000 a year to incarcerate a prisoner in California, compared to $3500 a year for education of schoolchildren. Now multiply that by the number of prison inmates - 2.3 million. The tab is enormous -- well over $60 billion. That's $600 per U.S. household each year! And that figure is a gross underestimate if you consider the costs to the incarcerated, their families and communities, resulting in a final cost estimate of $1 trillion.[121] In comparison, educating 2.3 million children, even in California, would only cost $8 billion.

Should we be trying harder to rehabilitate these people, so they can become productive, contributing members of society? Or do we really want to provide them free room and board behind bars at our expense?

It's certainly true that we have to lock up the worst in our society to keep them from harming us. But we have been doing too much of that, and too many of these criminals aren't the worst in our society. We've run out of prison space. We put offenders on probation because we can't afford to lock up any more. We're constantly constructing new prisons, and the prisoners we release keep on offending, winding back up in the slammer as recidivists (repeat offenders) in no time.

Former NYPD Commissioner Bernard Kerik laments about the "insane money our country wastes on incarcerating people who could be dealt with, punished in alternative ways."[122]

A badly needed 2015 bipartisan Sentencing Reform and Corrections Act failed to pass. Incarcerations must decrease. The high recidivism rate has to be lowered.

How to Improve the Prison and Correctional System

In the following section I want to focus on ways to improve the prison and correctional systems, reduce the number of prison inmates, and prepare them for successful re-entry back into society.

Currently those with the power to change the system are conservative suburbanites who have the least to do with the system, and therefore are the most unaware of its faults. This book represents an attempt to remedy that situation. For those who aren't familiar with the prison system and its inner workings, I want to provide an overview here of how the system works.

I am concerned that politicians of both stripes have allowed the system to evolve into the monstrosity it has become. Reform has to happen locally in the form of hundreds of grass roots movements, because so few of the incarcerated are under federal jurisdiction. This reform will be easiest to accomplish in states under one-party control, particularly in Republican-controlled states in the South and Midwest. In other parts of the country, it may take alliances between concerned citizens on the right (corporate and faith-based organizations) and the left (equal justice and civil rights advocates) to work together to fix the system.

Do we have a problem here? You bet we do. Do we have solutions? Yes, lots of them. They're in Part III, but we have to begin with how to lower recidivism (keep those being released from re-offending). To do that, we have to gain some insights from other countries to find out how they do some things better than we do.

PART III: SOLUTIONS

- **Lowering Recidivism**
- **Other Proposed Remedies**

CHAPTER 5: LOWERING RECIDIVISM

How Other Countries Deal with Prisons and Recidivism[123]

As already mentioned, one of the most shameful aspects of prisons in the U.S. is that we incarcerate a far higher proportion of our population than *any* other country, six times more than the average in Europe.

Unfortunately, our higher incarceration doesn't translate into lower crime statistics. For example, the U.S. murder rate is significantly higher than that of Western European countries, which have a considerably lower murder rate than that of the U.S.,[124] similar to the differences in incarceration rates.

What are the reasons for the lower incarceration rate and less crime in other countries? I'll provide some examples to illustrate in the next sections.

Examples of Prisons in Other Countries

Europe

While the U.S. represents one extreme of incarceration, **Norway** represents the opposite extreme. Guards there carry no weapons, prisoners wear no uniforms, and the courts are less punitive. Most Norwegian prisons seem like country clubs to us.[125]

They permit their inmates considerable freedom within the confines of the prison perimeter, allow them to cook their own meals, and provide them with considerable work training to prepare them for release. They even allow them to leave prison for work.

The prisons in Norway are small and located all around the country, and they allow prisoners to visit their families.[126] Their prison cells look like dorm rooms at a college.

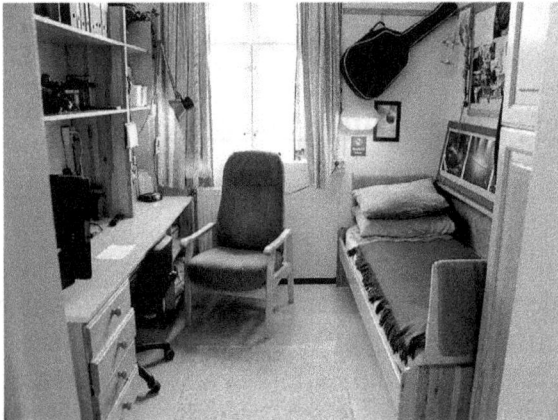

Norwegian prisons have these characteristics because the criminal justice system there emphasizes rehabilitation over punishment. The recidivism rate in Norway and the rest of Scandinavia is far lower than ours.

Under these less punitive conditions, it is easier for Scandinavian prisoners to take responsibility and blame themselves for their plight, rather than blaming other individuals, their disadvantages growing up, the prison environment, or society in general, as U.S. prisoners often do. Thus, Scandinavian prisoners are better able to express remorse and seek to change themselves to improve their lives upon release.[127]

Though Norway spends three times more money per prisoner than we do,[128] they find the cost well worth it. In the long run they have fewer re-offenders after release, thus fewer prisoners, and a greater contribution to society from ex-prisoners. However, it is unlikely that the U.S. public will see fit to triple spending on our criminals.

Prisons in **Germany** are more similar to the Scandinavian model than to ours. Fewer of those convicted are sent to prison. Only about 5% wind up in prison.[129] Many more prisoners receive sentences in the form of fines, which are assigned based in part on the offender's ability to pay. These fines keep them working. Up to one-third of the prisoners pay a "transaction" fee to avoid criminal prosecution, which has the same effect.[130]

Another big perk of the German prison system is that many of the prisoners are allowed out to work in the daytime and to visit friends and families several times a year.[131] Prison sentences are frequently suspended into a form of probation, and tasks are assigned similar to U.S. requirements for community service.[132] Of German prison sentences, 75% are for under one year, 92% are for under two years, and most of those terms are suspended. That's compared to an average prison sentence of three years or more in the U.S.[133] Germans with mental illness are sent to psychiatric hospitals rather than to prison.[134]

The Americas

Closer to home, both incarceration rates and violent crime rates are much lower in Canada than for us, more nearly like Western Europe.[135]

Canada experiences less than half the violent crime as the U.S.[136] and incarcerates fewer people. Part of the reason may be that there is basically no difference in violent crime rates between large urban centers in Canada and rural areas, in contrast to large urban centers in the U.S.[137,138,139,140] Unlike the extent of urban crime associated with black poverty in the U.S., Canada's black population is only about a quarter of that of the U.S., and no city over a half million has more than a 13.5% black population.[141]

Mean and median sentences for violent crimes are very much shorter in Canada[142] than in the U.S.[143] As the following table illustrates, the average sentence is only 10 months in Canada versus 71 to 97 months in the U.S. – about 7 to 9 times longer.

	Mean sentence in months
Canadian courts	10
U.S. state courts	71
U.S. large county courts	94
U.S. federal district courts	97

Evidently, shorter sentences in Canada have not led to violent crime rates as high as those in the U.S.

In the 1990's, Canada spent about $20 per citizen for legal aid (public defenders),[144] more than double what we spend.[145] This extra expense is cost-effective for them due to the lower rate of imprisonment they generate. Accordingly, what we can learn from this is that more adequate representation for the indigent would certainly help reduce the number of inappropriate plea deals and reduce the casework overload of U.S. public defenders. Better defense representation would be less costly than more trials.

The clearance rate[146] for violent crime in Canada is about 72%,[147] much higher than the 46.8% reported in the U.S.[148] More serious police detective work might help reduce crime statistics and take the guilty off the streets.

Restorative justice programs in Canada have been shown to reduce recidivism by almost one-half. These programs require convicts to apologize to their victims, work to provide restitution to their victims, and perform community service.

These examples from Canada offer some alternatives we might try in the U.S. to reduce both our rates of incarceration and returns to prison.

Asia

Australia has prisoners work offsite to provide reparations to the community. In addition, Australia has humane private prisons which help to prepare their "residents" for release in private pre-release centers.[149] The "residents" go to school and farm on-site or work off-site providing reparations to the outside community, where they also go to alcoholics anonymous and narcotics anonymous meetings. Female residents get to see their children regularly. The private prisons are run by a Serco, a company with a $10 billion dollar portfolio, a staff of 100,000 and contracts in 30 countries. Their contracts include recidivism-based measures as incentives. Thus private prisons can be very humane and even save money over their government-run counterparts.

Singapore managed to reduce its recidivism rate from 40% in 2000 down to 23.6% in 2010 by helping convicts leaving prison find jobs. Singapore inmates enjoy a staggering 99% success rate in finding jobs in the food, beverage, retail, or tourism industries. Prisoners do most of the baking for their airlines and laundry for their hospitals. The prison provides help in finding the jobs and provides the needed training. Singapore emphasizes punishment much more than in Europe, such as by making inmates sleep on straw mats and keeping them locked up in cells 23 hours a day for the first tenth of their sentences. However, the prisons prepare their convicts for release by requiring them to participate in rehabilitation.

Summing Up[150]

Although the methods of defining and counting recidivism vary from country to country, making comparison difficult,[151] we can still learn from other countries many ways to improve prison practices here:

- ❖ **observations**
- ➢ **recommendations**

- ❖ When properly implemented, treating prisoners with more respect and humanity succeeds in getting them to take responsibility for their actions instead of blaming "the system" that incarcerated them.

- ❖ An emphasis on rehabilitation helps more than the current U.S. emphasis on punishment. Rehabilitation reduces recidivism and results in a calmer, more peaceful prison environment, less likely to result in fights or riots.

    - ➢ We should increase the emphasis on rehabilitation as opposed to punishment.

- ❖ Shorter sentence lengths can reduce over-incarceration.

- ❖ Hiring more public defenders to prevent inappropriate plea deals would also reduce incarceration.

- ❖ Solving crimes at a higher clearance rate with more detectives might help reduce crime.

> Prisoners should be instructed in a trade in order to make them much more employable upon release.

How Oregon and New York City Have Dealt with Prisons and Recidivism[152]

How Oregon Reduced Recidivism

A Pew Center study concluded that Oregon was a standout compared to other states in reducing recidivism by its more prisoner-supportive policies coupled with fair but firm sanctions for parole violations.

Perhaps the biggest change Oregon instituted was that it virtually eliminated sending certain parole violators back to prison, those that had only committed a technical violation of their parole conditions rather than committing a new crime. Instead, the Oregon parole system generated a graduated series of sanctions for technical violations of parole, including a fine or a short jail stay to hold parole violators accountable.

New York City: Does It Offer Tips to Reduce Incarceration Without Increasing Crime?

New York City had a very high violent crime rate that reduced rapidly after its peak in 1991, and incarceration actually declined over most of that time, unlike incarceration in the country as a whole.

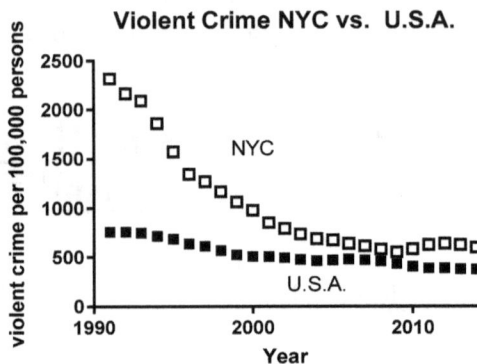

Violent Crime NYC vs. U.S.A.

(y-axis) violent crime per 100,000 persons — 0, 500, 1000, 1500, 2000, 2500

NYC

U.S.A.

(x-axis) Year — 1990, 2000, 2010

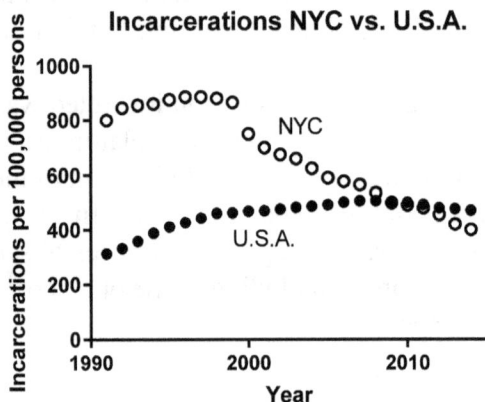

Incarcerations NYC vs. U.S.A.

(y-axis) Incarcerations per 100,000 persons — 0, 200, 400, 600, 800, 1000

NYC

U.S.A.

(x-axis) Year — 1990, 2000, 2010

Correlation analysis presented in my book *The Costly U.S. Prison System* suggested there were three major factors contributing to Reducing Violent Crime in NYC at different points in time:

1) **Reducing Recidivism** (1991-2011)

2) **Increasing Incarceration** (1991-1997)

3) **Increasing Police Staffing** (1980-2002)

Lessons to be drawn from NYC

So what policies might have reduced crime, especially without increasing incarceration? Certainly, some policies have had more effect than others in New York City. However, complicating matters is the fact that a policy may be effective during one time period, but then it may become less effective for any number of reasons.

Then, too, policies that may have an impact in one city may not in another city or state due to differing conditions in different areas. Still, some of the policies that worked in New York City to reduce both crime and incarceration should be among the first to be tried in other cities. Thus, some policies to try out first might be:

(2 of 4 recommendations in this section of *The Costly U.S. Prison System* are shown here)

➢ Reduce recidivism, particularly by reducing imprisonment for technical violators of parole.

➢ Increase imprisonment when violent crime is very high.

Conclusions

One lesson to be learned from comparisons of prison policy between states or cities, as with comparisons between countries discussed previously, is that rehabilitation can be used to reduce recidivism. However, the degree of success depends on a number of factors. These include a supportive environment from guards and other prisoners, a willingness of the prisoner to change, and an openness of local company employers to be receptive to providing a job to a prisoner on probation, parole, or just released from prison, as will be discussed further in the next chapter.

We have seen that Oregon and New York City both managed to reduce incarceration by reducing recidivism. Oregon did so by reducing imprisonment for technical violations of parole, whereas New York City reduced recidivism by reducing the commitment of new felonies by ex-offenders. Imagine what could happen if both effects could be effected somewhere at the same time. Or suppose that somewhere could be nationwide. That could really lead to less incarceration, less cost and less crime!

In summary, policy in different states and cities suggests the following[153]:

❖ **observations**
➢ **recommendations**

❖ When properly implemented, an emphasis on rehabilitation can result in shorter sentences, less recidivism, and considerable savings.

    ➢ Reduce recidivism, starting by reducing imprisonment for technical violators of parole or probation. Reducing recidivism is key.

❖ In urban settings, more police officers on the beat may act as another deterrent to crime, even if the police don't make additional stops or arrests.

    ➢ Increase the number of police officers assigned to a targeted high crime area.

Reducing Recidivism[154]

Reducing recidivism is a key way to both reduce crime and costs, so any strategies to reduce recidivism, even if more costly in the near term, can be much more cost effective in the long term.

One key to achieving less recidivism is helping ex-cons adjust to life outside prison. President George W. Bush pointed this out in his 2004 State of the Union Address, when he spoke about the difficulty that ex-cons have in adjusting to life outside of prison, resulting in a high rate of recidivism. As he stated:

"This year, some 600,000 inmates will be released from prison back into society. We know from long experience that if they can't find work, or a home, or help, they are much more likely to commit more crimes and return to prison.... America is the land of the second chance, and when the gates of the prison open, the path ahead should lead to a better life."[155]

But unfortunately, the path ahead does not usually lead to this better life; instead the ex-con is confronted with difficult barriers to remaining out of prison at every turn. A key reason for this difficulty is the kind of mental transformation that a prisoner experiences when placed in confinement, and the longer the prison term, the more the prisoner experiences this negative impact on his thinking and identity.

Former NYPD Commissioner Bernard Kerik stated this dilemma well when he observed that: "Taking away someone's freedom is mind altering. Your objective should not be to treat these individuals like animals but to prepare them for reintegration into society."[156] Kerik should know, because he's been on both sides of the bars, having served as NYPD Commissioner, but then pleading guilty to filing false tax returns and lying to the White House, for which he was imprisoned.

Doing something about recidivism now is extremely important, because recidivism in the U.S. is very high and increasing -- and incarceration and associated costs cannot be reduced long term unless the recidivism rates go down. The alarming increase in recidivism is shown by a recent study on Minnesota prisoners, which determined that the average offender in 1981 had 1 prior felony conviction, whereas similar offenders in 1991 had 2, and ones in 2013 had 2.5 felony convictions.[157] Clearly, ex-convicts are re-offending at a rapidly increasing rate that can and must be reversed.

Reducing recidivism is critical, because it is one of the keys to reducing our mass incarceration dilemma. Almost half of those entering prison are ex-cons. A 2007 Department of Justice report concluded that incarceration actually increases offender recidivism.[158] Most prisoners who are released wind up arrested and back in prison because they are ill prepared to deal with the outside world. According to Bureau of Justice statistics, the re-arrest rate for prisoners released in 30 states in 2005 was 57% within one year, 68% within three years, and 77% for the first five years following release. Statistics show that the first year is when the most recidivism occurs, so this is when intervention is most needed to help the ex-con have a successful re-entry. The first year is the time when a newly released convict faces the most difficulty in adjusting to the world outside prison, which can include finding a job, reconnecting with family members, and learning about new changes in technology and society that require adjustment. If the ex-con is able to successfully navigate these new experiences on leaving prison in this first critical year, he or she will be more likely to continue to find success in this new environment, so recidivism later on becomes less likely. But if the ex-con is unable to find the needed assistance or land a job in that critical first year, that failure can set him or her on the path to reconnecting with old criminal buddies or committing crimes again to get the money to survive.

Still another reason way to reduce the high rate of recidivism is to eliminate sending ex-cons back to prison for technical violations of parole, unless these violations are accompanied by other criminal behavior. Technical violations account for approximately one-third of the returns to prison,[159] as John Pfaff concluded in *Locked In,* based on conducting dozens of interviews with recidivists.[160] Sending minor infraction technical violators of parole back to prison clearly increases the costs of incarceration, and these could easily be handled through less costly community-based penalties.

Many technical violations can be quite innocuous activities, such as forgetting to contact a parole or probation officer or not having access to a phone to make a check-in call. Other violations might be a prohibited meeting with an old girlfriend who drops by the house or going to a local baseball game where former gang members are present, even though the ex-con has no personal contact with them. Parole and probation officers may take a hard line on such infractions, so rather than give an ex-con a warning, fine, or another chance to stick to the rules in the future, the ex-con may simply be sent back to the slammer.

Some Reasons for High Recidivism

One big problem that prisoners face when they are released is the lack of preparedness and support they receive upon getting out to a world without the extensive structure they have grown accustomed to in prison. This lack of preparedness and support contributes to the high recidivism rate. While ex-cons are also subject to many confining rules and regulations ordinary citizens would find abhorrent, those rules and regulations may actually provide them some structure that they find missing when released. If they have help in changing their behaviors and better adjusting to the world outside on release, they will be more successful in avoiding a return to prison.

Prisoners who are adjusted to prison life, where they have little or no freedom and no responsibility, have to swiftly readjust to a system where they have both.

Commonly, many are put on parole long-term and required to stay for several months in halfway houses. There they learn some reentry skills and get some assistance in obtaining initial employment. But the jobs they get are minimum wage, and their wages are paid to the halfway houses and frequently garnished.

Their parole officer can make unannounced visits. If guns, alcohol or drugs are found in the household they are staying in, even if these items are not theirs, they generally get hauled off back to prison for technical violation of their parole. This happens to about one-third of all parolees.[199,161] Meanwhile, many, if not most inmates have been forgotten and forsaken by their families, and all their possessions have disappeared.

- ❖ felons cannot receive federal housing, and
- ❖ felons most often must divulge that they have been to prison to potential employers, and this admission greatly decreases their job prospects,[162] since many prospective employers fear becoming a victim of ex-cons.

Employment substantially reduces the risk of recidivism. Yet more than 60% of ex-cons remain jobless their first year after release,[163] their most vulnerable time for committing a crime or a violation of their release which will send them back to prison.

Reducing Recidivism Reduces Incarceration

A good way to reduce recidivism is to simply reduce the incarceration of ex-convicts for minor technical violations of parole which could be handled by warnings and fines.

If less severe sanctions were imposed for technical violations of parole, this could reduce recidivism by one-third,[164] and that change in policy would have a major effect to reduce the number of incarcerated.

Reductions in recidivism alone can make a substantial dent on our prison population. That's because over 600,000 prisoners are released each year and 55% of them re-offend within five years.[165] The following chart indicates how reducing recidivism by one-third (as by eliminating imprisoning technical violators of parole) can decrease the prison population by about 300,000 in five years all by itself.

**Effect of Reducing Recidivism
on Prison Population**

no reduction in recidivism

33% reduction in recidivism

Millions imprisoned

1.5

1.0

0.5

0.0

0   1   2   3   4   5

Years from present

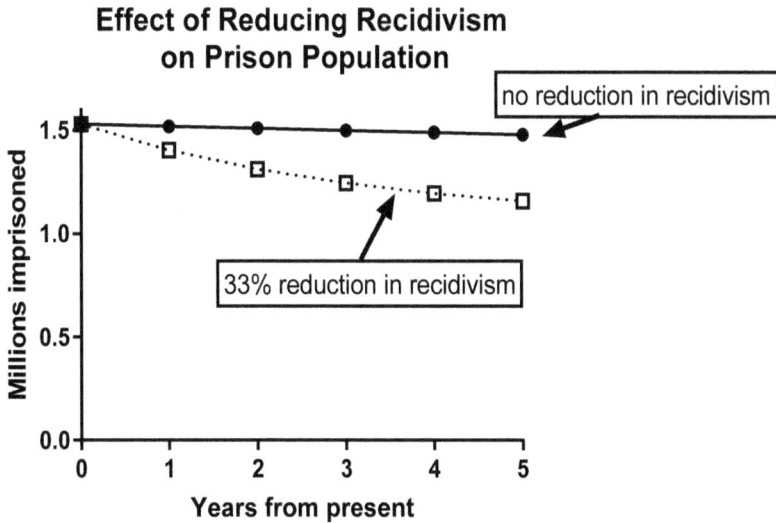

Translated into money saved, that reduction in incarceration could represent $15-20 billion a year[166] out of the costs of upkeep for those individuals unnecessarily imprisoned. Lowering recidivism would save untold billions more by staunching the loss of their productivity and lowering the cost to the family and community due to crimes committed by the released prisoners.

Some Ways to Reduce Recidivism

There are several approaches that have been found to work, and I will describe them here, together with new approaches that should work.

Providing training in prison was the key to reducing recidivism, according to a 2013 RAND Corporation report.[167] Their findings suggested that each $1 invested in prison education saved $4-$5 in incarceration costs in the first three years following release. This investment involved spending only about $1600 per inmate, a minor additional cost relative to the $20,000-$30,000 yearly cost of imprisoning one inmate.

The results were spectacular. Inmates participating in education programs reduced their odds of returning to prison by 43%.

Current Programs Aimed at Reducing Recidivism

Many other programs are described in *The Costly U.S. Prison System*. Some programs are faith-based, some are apolitical, and others involve alliances between corporate donors and liberal social workers. For instance, Koch Industries, a conservative industry group much maligned by liberals, came together with the ACLU[168] to promote overhauling the criminal justice system, under the group's name: the Coalition for Public Safety.

It is refreshing that groups like Koch Industries on the right and ACLU on the left can work together more constructively than our elected politicians. Perhaps compromise is not extinct after all, merely on the list of endangered species. Political and public discourse in the U.S. has been squeezed into sound bites, tweets and slogans which divide us too much, sometimes in seemingly contradictory ways.[169]

There are many small rehabilitation programs in many communities. Though these are individually small programs, they add up, resulting in potentially thousands of ex-convicts that benefit from such programs each year. And the more lives that are touched by such programs, the less likely these ex-convicts are to commit new crimes and return to prison.

Legislation Dealing with Recidivism

Aside from ongoing programs, a number of states have passed legislation aimed at reducing recidivism. For example, in Arkansas, in April 2017, the state legislature passed Act 423, the Criminal Justice Efficiency and Safety Act.

One big positive is that the act replaces sending ex-cons with technical violations of parole and probation to prison by instead sending them to Arkansas Community Correction facilities for 45 to 90 days for rehabilitative programming.

Conservative legislators are giving this legislation favoring rehabilitation a strong endorsement, given its ability to reduce costs and crime.

Summing Up

In summary, the main observation I have made and the changes I suggest making are these[170]:

- ❖ **observation**
- ➤ **recommendations**

- ❖ Many local programs have been implemented that seem to reduce recidivism.

  - ➤ These local programs need to be promoted and then evaluated and compared on a cost-effectiveness basis as best as possible to determine which are the most effective in reducing recidivism.

  - ➤ Those programs that are the most effective should be expanded with local, state, and/or federal support.

If we can make these changes in the current status of prison management, we should be able to achieve the following:

  - ➤ Have many more ex-convicts re-enter society as productive individuals.

If these developments can be implemented, that would represent a win-win situation for not only the prisoners and their families, but for society as a whole, especially for conservatives like ourselves. This is because the costs for imprisonment will decrease while simultaneously reducing crime and generating greater economic contribution to society from ex-cons.

CHAPTER 6: OTHER PROPOSED REMEDIES

More Ways to Reduce Incarceration[171]

As the previous chapter has illustrated, we can reduce recidivism by not sending technical violators of parole back to prison. But that strategy alone won't fix the problem. It is likely that several different solutions have to be imposed to fix our massive problem of over-incarceration. Before proposing all sorts of possible solutions, we should consider two things:

1) Who is in the best position to correct the problem without significant increases in costs?

2) What factors might contribute to or limit any practical implementation of such proposed solutions?

Then, we can select the approaches that should be the most effective in reducing incarceration.

Should the Feds Take the Lead or States and Counties?

Given these problems of over-incarceration in both state and federal prisons, the next question is what to do about it, and what is the best level of government to lead this effort. In general, the states should lead the charge.

The reason the states should take the lead is because state prisons with their larger prison population account for the vast majority of the increase in incarceration. Since most prisoners are in state prisons, states are footing the bill for most prisoners right now, as well as spending more on other correction strategies -- far outpacing what the federal government spends. These patterns are illustrated in the chart on page 81, which shows how much more incarceration occurs in state prisons than federal ones, costing states much more than the federal government.[172]

The Role Conservatives Can Play in Fixing the System

Local conservatives are in an increasingly powerful position to take the lead in fixing the criminal justice system, including reducing unnecessary incarcerations and the excess costs associated with them. In the South and Midwest, conservatives control state governments. Moreover, the current national leadership, supported by the conservative media, is contributing to the growing strength of the local movements. So conservatives take heart!

The growing conservative national leadership for criminal justice reform includes such powerful figures in politics, industry, and the media as Newt Gingrich, Grover Nordquist, the conservative lobbyist who has congressmen sign pledges to support no new taxes, the Koch brothers, Rand Paul, and the libertarian Cato Institute. These conservatives, plus many others, have been offering their public support for efforts to fix the criminal justice system with a view toward making it operate more efficiently and at a lower cost. For example, in 2010, Gingrich and former California legislator Pat Nolan published an op-ed in the *Washington Post* stating that "the criminal justice system is broken and conservatives must lead the way in fixing it." Conservatives have also publicly endorsed the use of faith-based initiatives to turn around the lives of convicted criminals who have previously been deemed incorrigible.

These new conservative voices supporting criminal justice reform represent a major change, since this growing movement enables conservatives to take the lead in shaping the national agenda and proposing conservative solutions to what has long been a costly, seemingly insoluble problem. In the past, the issue of crime reduction has been regarded by the general public and media as an issue "owned" by liberals,[173] whose approach to most crime problems has been to advocate fewer laws and lesser penalties for crime. In other words, their approach has been to tamp down the definition of what is a crime or a criminal in the interest of fewer

126

penalties, consistent with their popular designation as "bleeding hearts."

A conservative approach can work well in the South, which has the highest incarceration rates of any region of the country and is solidly red.

Incentives for Increasing or Decreasing Incarcerations

Keeping the public safe from criminals is the primary incentive for increasing incarcerations.

By comparison, cost savings is the primary incentive for decreasing incarceration, especially for conservatives.

The political cost of locking up even several innocent people appears to be quite small relative to the cost of making one mistake by releasing a parolee who goes on to commit another heinous crime.[174]

Under the circumstances, reducing the influence of elected officials on the process of making decisions about the everyday operations of the correctional systems might help reduce incarceration. Pfaff, who attributes much of our economic burden of incarceration to prosecutors, suggests appointing prosecutors and judges. As opposed to electing them, appointments shield political officials from the influence of the public,[175] since under the influence of the media, the public perceives that crime is always rising, even when it is really falling.[176]

Another prosecutor-related incentive for increasing incarceration is that the vast majority of prosecutors are county prosecutors, and they send more prisoners to state prisons than to county jails. Consequently, the counties who pay the prosecutors don't have to foot the bill for the prosecutors' actions, and the prosecutors feel no consequences for locking up more people. Instead, the states pay for the incarceration, though they have little control or oversight over the process.[177] Incentives to decrease incarceration must be made to surpass incentives for prosecutors to increase incarceration.

Measures to be Considered

Longer incarceration is a less effective deterrent to crime than the certainty of punishment.[178] Unfortunately, the prospect for punishment is not at all certain, since the police only solve about two thirds of murders and about half of aggravated assault cases. And the likelihood of solving the case is even less for property crimes, since the police only solve 13-14% of burglaries and auto thefts. On the other hand, when individuals are tested for drugs and immediately penalized with sanctions that are not too severe, there is a great reduction in recidivism.

That's what happened for "Swift, Certain and Fair," an around-the-country outgrowth of Hawaii's Opportunity Probation with Enforcement (HOPE) program. HOPE tests for drugs daily and imposes immediate short term jail sanctions of a few days that are not too severe, resulting in improved outcomes. After one year, only 21% of participants in the HOPE program were rearrested compared to 47% of non-participants. They were incarcerated only about half as many days and had a radically lower rate of positive drug testing, 13% vs. 46%.[179,180]

Juveniles Should Not Be Imprisoned Together with Seasoned Adult Criminals

Long-time Republican law and order advocate Bernard Kerik points to the dangers of long sentences with youthful offenders. As he asserts: "If we do not shorten their sentences....we may as well sentence them to life in prison or death."[181] The reason for this outcome is that a long-term prison sentence exposes the juvenile offender to a virtual school for crime, as he or she learns different crime techniques from seasoned criminals who serve as mentors.

Reducing the Number and Length of Incarcerations

Alternatives to prison, such as probation, electronic monitoring, substance abuse and mental health treatment, community service, and fines, should all be more seriously considered in cases of nonviolent crimes.

The liberal Brennan Center for Justice recommends a 25% reduction in prison sentence lengths for nonviolent crimes. This particular liberal recommendation might actually reduce economic costs.

Another way to reduce incarcerations for non-violent prisoners is to tie a reduction in a sentence to participation in skills training or getting an educational degree. The advantage here is giving the individual convicted of a crime an opportunity to learn better job skills that can lead to employment outside of prison and a decline in subsequent criminality. This is an approach that was implemented by corrections officials in California.

Another Initial Fix to Reduce Incarceration

The Brennan Center has estimated that 39% of the prison population could be released without significantly impacting public safety.[182] The Center claims this release is justified because some of the crimes were so minor and non-violent that they should not have led to incarceration in the first place (25%) or because the time already served by the prisoner would constitute a just sentence (14%).

Most of the 39% released will probably become recidivists unless something else is done to address that. If you simultaneously reduce recidivism by 33% by eliminating imprisonment for technical violations of parole, then the reduction in imprisonment is much greater and maintained much longer.

Most people don't realize that almost 42% of all prisoners are released annually already, but 55% of them wind up back in prison due to recidivism. Accordingly, I recommend the following:

> ➢ Any release should be delayed a year to permit sufficient rehabilitation training for those to be released.
> ➢ Approximately 10% of the inmates should be released each year over the next four years, which will eventually accomplish the 39% release, only more gradually, as illustrated on the chart below.

As this chart shows, at the current rate, approximately 1.5 million will remain in prison in five years. There is a modest reduction in prisoners if 39% are released in a delayed and incremental fashion, but a much more significant decrease if the release is accompanied by a 33% reduction in recidivism. All told, the prison population could be reduced by over one-third, to less than 1 million within 5 years.

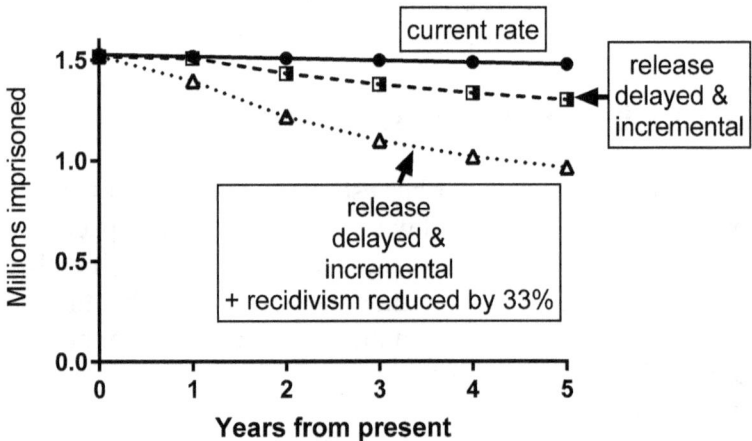

Measures Requiring More Time to Reduce Incarceration[183]

> ➢ Greater funds should be provided for defense attorneys for indigent defendants.[184] Providing these finds is needed, since 80% of people charged with crimes cannot afford a defense attorney, and they aren't provided with an adequate

defense by beleaguered public defenders.[185] A good reason for improving their defense abilities is that 95% of defendants end up taking a plea deal. That's because defendants without the financial means to afford an attorney to fight for them may feel they have little choice but to plead guilty and accept a reduced sentence rather than risk — and likely receive — a much longer punishment. Many even admit to crimes they are not responsible for committing. With a better defense, many defendants accused of non-violent crimes could be guided into rehabilitative programs that would reduce their likelihood of engaging in criminal activity again. The current *pro bono* system should be expanded with sufficient funds to encourage new lawyers to come to the aid of financially strapped clients. This system, in turn, would provide an outlet for attorneys who are having difficulty finding employment.

➢ Establish addiction treatment centers in major cities, since treatment at these centers is likely to result in the successful reentry of many former addicts back into society. These centers would be staffed by a team of psychologists, social workers, and medical professionals with an expertise in addiction problems. Ex-convicts with addictions would be required to go to regular support group meetings, along with individual meetings with an assigned counselor. Such ex-convicts would also be regularly monitored through urine testing protocols in order to determine if the program is working for them. If not, additional treatment approaches might be added. While the costs of such treatment might seem high, the ex-con addict would probably only require treatment for a few months, resulting in major long-term savings compared to imprisonment. The program would not need to be extended beyond a few months for those who are not helped.

Longer Term Approaches to Reduce Incarcerations[186]

- Incentivize private prisons by paying them based on how their prisoners perform after release, as in Australia. This would be similar to suggestions to improve healthcare by incentivizing medical groups to pay for improved health outcomes for their patients, rather than allowing them to charge fees for each service rendered. Currently prisons are paid based on how many prisoners they house, and if a former prisoner returns, the private prison profits.[187] Private prisons can respond much more quickly to mandates or incentives to make changes, whereas public prisons depend on the passage of legislation or some public approval process, which could be difficult in these divisive times. Therefore, it would make more sense to enroll and incentivize private prisons properly in order to give prisoners the tools they need to better readjust when they are released.

- Prosecutors should be appointed rather than elected, because that would diminish the influence of the demands of the public for public safety, which has led to over-incarceration.[188]

- A financial realignment should be made to shift imprisonment costs to the counties that pay prosecutors, making prosecutors more financially responsible. Prosecutors currently are under no pressure to keep costs down, because states foot the bill for the prisoners that prosecutors convict. If necessary, this new policy could require each county to be assigned a cap on the number of inmates it could send to state prisons, with any county having to buy prison "beds" from other counties if they exceed their cap.[189]

A Fix to Reduce the Numbers of Arrestees in Jail

Bail bonds currently represent a for-profit industry that is found only in the U.S. and the Philippines.[190] Bail bond policy costs arrestees, primarily poor ones, 14 billion dollars a year by throwing them in jail. The vast majority of arrestees cannot afford to post bond themselves. Bail bonds represent a contract with bail bondsmen, in which the bail paid cannot be recovered and is frequently paid in installments with interest amounting to $1.4-2.4 billion annually.[191] A portion of the profit goes to a small number of bail insurance corporations. Meanwhile, each jailed convict costs the county over $26,000 a year to be housed[192], while his or her life implodes in jail, and any income from a job on hold or terminated is lost to the community and taxpayers, too.

More than 60% of America's jail population has not been convicted. Remaining in jail because they can't afford to post bail causes many arrestees to accept plea deals just to end their in limbo status while waiting for their day in court, even if they were innocent. Otherwise, many languish in jail for months before any trial and verdict. When finally released, they may find their job, housing, property, spouse, and/or children already gone. The acceptance of these plea deals and the negative consequences of accepting them are reflected in increased conviction rates for those who can't afford bail versus those who can.

> ➤ Reform the bail bond system[193] by returning to the 1966 Bail Reform Act which requires using the least restrictive lower bail approach to ensure an arrestee shows up in court rather than confining him in jail.[194] This would be a more reasonable and cost-effective approach in that over 60% of those in jail have not been convicted and are in pretrial detention.[195] Such an approach would certainly reduce the numbers of arrestees in jail, though it would not have much impact on the prison population.

Other Measures to Reduce Incarcerations

Actions to Take at the Initial Point of Contact with the System[196]

- ➤ Issue citations instead of arrests for minor cases.

- ➤ Stop sentencing minor drug violation offenders to prison.

- ➤ Make electronic monitoring the legal equivalent of incarceration for prisoners involved in less serious and non-violent crimes.

- ➤ Offer diversion programs such as mental health courts and drug courts instead of incarceration.

- ➤ Eliminate or reduce technical violations of parole or probation.

- ➤ Reduce recidivism by no longer sending technical violators of parole back to prison.

Long-Term Prevention/Community Development Strategies[197]

- ➤ Increase education and job training for people in prison.

- ➤ Retrain police so they have more racial/ethnic/gender sensitivity and better understand use of force guidelines, restorative practices, and when to call for mental health crisis intervention.

- ➤ Populate mental hospitals and psych wards with properly trained staff, so mentally ill prisoners can be sent there as an alternative to jail and prison.

Prison/Jail/Court Practices and Policies

> ➢ Create incentives for early release, such as by allowing offers of employment to qualify the prisoner for early release.

> ➢ Increase the use of community corrections programs, such as work release and work furlough.

> ➢ Retrain court and prison officials so they are more sensitive to prisoners from different racial, ethnic, and gender backgrounds.

> ➢ Increase the compassionate release of elderly, disabled, or extremely ill prisoners who have not committed serious crimes.

Legislative Changes

> ➢ Decriminalize drug possession.

> ➢ Reduce or eliminate criminal justice fines as a source of income for the government.

> ➢ Reduce barriers to employment and to benefits for people with felony convictions by dropping certain less serious crimes from public records, while leaving them available for law enforcement and court records.

> ➢ Shorten the terms of parole.

> ➢ Reduce or eliminate harsh sentencing policies, such as mandatory minimums, three strikes laws, and truth in sentencing, while insisting that at least 80% of a sentence

be served. Alternatively, allow greater judicial flexibility in their application in order to reduce or eliminate unnecessary incarcerations.

Two Prescriptions to Fix Our Broken Criminal Justice System[198]

How else can we fix our broken criminal justice system? The first prescription is my own suggestion. The other involves an effort that goes back almost a decade, if not longer.

Prescription: Separate Courts for Urban, Suburban and Rural Areas

Separate courts in urban, suburban, and rural areas would bring more justice to the criminal justice system because of the differences in conditions and perspectives in these different areas. Residents in each area also are unaware of these differences. Most suburban voters in middle and upper income neighborhoods have little idea of ongoing abuses in the criminal justice system. Rural voters are similarly unaware of the abuses, since they are less likely to be affected by high crime rates. Thus, for suburban and rural constituencies alike, the criminal justice system seemingly operates in another universe: one comprising the inner cities.

William J. Stuntz, an evangelical Christian and avowed conservative at Harvard Law School, claimed in *The Collapse of American Criminal Justice* that, "the American system of criminal justice has unraveled before our eyes — a phenomenon that has escaped the notice of most citizens."[199] In Stuntz's view, this lack of awareness among the general population occurred because the middle and upper classes live separate and apart from the urban poor, who are the primary targets of the criminal justice system's machinery.[133]

When those in the middle and upper classes think about how the criminal justice system works, they draw on a misleading picture presented by TV and the movies, which glamorize the police, investigators, and prosecutors. These TV law enforcement professionals score a win when they solve the crime and toss the criminal in jail, and virtually all criminals depicted on these shows are guilty, so the system itself is never at fault. These dramas, suspense thrillers, and action/adventure shows typically try to avoid the stereotypes that fuel racial discrimination by featuring criminals from different social classes -- and often white middle and upper class criminals have starring roles. By contrast, such discrimination is rampant in the real day-to-day criminal justice system. The stories are unrealistic in that they do not depict the real long and drawn-out process and bureaucratic nightmare that confronts a primarily poor, inner city defendant, since crimes are typically solved in a single 30 to 60 minute TV episode.

➢ Separate jurisdictions might also have separate slates of prosecutors and judges, so citizens vote only for the prosecutors and judges for their area.

➢ The use of separate courts in different jurisdictions might contribute to both reductions in sentences and less incarceration. For example, judges in a local area might be more receptive to consider alternative sentences like halfway houses or probation rather than incarcerations.

Prescription: Overhaul the Criminal Justice System

In March 2009, Senator James Webb issued a call for a national commission to completely overhaul the system -- a commission vitally needed now more than ever. In particular, the commission should find answers to these key questions raised by Senator Webb:

- ❖ Why are so many more Americans in prison compared with other countries and with ourselves just 50 years ago?
- ❖ What do our current prison and criminal justice policies cost our nation in lost tax dollars?
- ❖ How can we better change our nation's drug policies?
- ❖ How can we better end violence in our prisons and on our city streets?
- ❖ How can we more effectively diagnose and treat mental illness, since so many of our prisoners, drug addicts, and homeless individuals are mentally ill?
- ❖ How can we create effective re-entry programs, so our communities can assimilate former offenders and encourage them to become productive citizens?
- ❖ How can we protect ourselves against the growing violence of internationally based gangs, which are spreading through our cities?[200]

A complete overhaul of the criminal justice system is needed, as reflected in a bill to do just this, which was introduced in 2009 by former Senator Jim Webb but unfortunately failed. Among his many reasons for introducing this bill are these huge figures, which show how expensive and ineffective our criminal justice system really is:

- ❖ The number of incarcerated drug offenders has soared 1,200% since 1980.

- ❖ Four times as many mentally ill people are in prisons as in mental health hospitals.

- ❖ Approximately 1 million gang members reside in the U.S., many of them foreign-based, and Mexican cartels operate in more than 230 communities across the country.

❖ Post-incarceration re-entry programs are haphazard and often nonexistent, making it extremely difficult for ex-offenders to become full, contributing members of society.

Such statistics are what led Senator Webb to author his National Criminal Justice Commission Act (S. 306) to effect the following reforms. He sought to:
"Create a blue-ribbon commission to look at every aspect of our criminal justice system with an eye toward reshaping the criminal justice system from top to bottom."[201]

Webb's proposed bill was designed to create the first comprehensive national review of crime policy in 45 years. However, the bill fell a mere three votes short of obtaining a supermajority (sixty votes) required for passage.[202]
Webb's bill became a victim of partisan gridlock. What should be done now? How can we do it better? How can we come up with legislation that actually passes? There appears to be an opening.
Liberals may have gotten the "jump" on conservatives on this issue, but conservatives are finally catching up. Before his retirement, Supreme Court Justice Anthony Kennedy, an appointee of Ronald Reagan, testified before a Financial Services and General Government Subcommittee, where he stated that "this idea of total incarceration just isn't working." Further, he stated that "California, my home state, had 187,000 people in jail, at a cost of over $30,000 a prisoner, compared to the amount they gave to schoolchildren; that's about $3,500 a year."[203]
Businessman Charles Koch, oft pilloried by liberals, has supported this pressing need for criminal justice reform, too. As he has concluded:

"Reversing over-criminalization and mass incarceration will improve societal well-being in many respects, most notably by decreasing poverty. Today, approximately 50 million people (about 14 percent of the population) are at or below the U.S. poverty rate. Fixing our criminal system could reduce the overall poverty rate as much as 30%, dramatically improving the quality of life throughout society — especially for the disadvantaged."[204]

Most tellingly, the conservative Heritage Foundation identifies a number of examples of overcriminalization and concludes:

❖ "Criminal justice reform is about more than policy debates in Congress or legal procedure; it is about how the lives and fortunes of ordinary Americans are threatened by abuse of the law. The criminal justice reform movement should focus on telling the stories of those who are affected by an overly zealous government and the excessive power of the state.

❖ Only by identifying the problem and highlighting why it matters will any meaningful change take place. Over-criminalization is not an easy problem to solve, but it is one that demands our attention."[205]

Perhaps recent across-the-aisle alliances, such as those involving Senators Mike Lee (R), Dick Durbin (D), Ted Cruz (R), Patrick Leahy (D), Cory Booker (D) and Rand Paul (R)[206,207] could put such a plan forward. Support from other conservative Senators and conservative Congressmen in the House should be encouraged. A 2018 initiative advanced by Presidential Advisor Jared Kushner appears to have been stymied by Attorney General Sessions, but it might be revived in the future.

However, reducing mass incarceration cannot just be a federal effort. States have to be involved, too, since "90% of those incarcerated are in state or local facilities....mass incarceration needs to be dismantled one state at a time."[208]

Thus, clearly there is a major role here for states' rights. States whose legislatures are reliably conservative or reliably liberal can most easily effect change in policy without jeopardizing their political future.

> Legislatures in those states should take up the mantle of criminal justice reform. They should reduce the bloated prison population by revising sentencing guidelines to reduce sentences or permit greater judicial discretion in sentencing. They should also provide further support for programs designed to train inmates for successful re-entry into society.

> Other states should make attempts at bipartisan criminal justice reform.

Such efforts to accomplish significant criminal justice reform are essential to implement now, while it is still possible to create change politically. Otherwise, the danger is that liberal activists may convince defendants to take truly radical action to crash the system. For example, Michelle Alexander has suggested defendants opt to go to trial rather than taking pleas, and if enough defendants choose this option, then the courts will be overwhelmed and the criminal justice system will literally grind to a halt.[209]

Reducing Violent Crime by Relieving Black Urban Poverty[210]

Since violent crime correlates with black urban poverty, it seems likely that more onerous police tactics to intimidate young black males will generate a pressure cooker situation that may easily lead to race riots and more fearfulness.

Thus, since young black males are the source of much violent crime, something needs to be done to reduce this. One solution is to get rid of the incentive to turn to crime by offering more job opportunities. This will require more job training, which can be provided by local companies. Additionally, supermarket chains could make a serious effort to locate stores in many poorly served minority neighborhoods and hire rehabilitated ex-cons to staff them. In addition, young black males must be given better role models than wealthy black athletes, drug dealers and pimps. Being an athlete offers an opportunity for only a very tiny number of individuals, and the other role models, while lucrative, are illegal and generate a likely path to ending up in prison. Furthermore, these occupations will only provide a living for a very small number of individuals.

The Role of Role Models and Inspirational Models

Unfortunately, many role models have proved to offer false hope. One former role model, OJ Simpson, imploded. Other black athletes have demonstrated terrible behavior toward women. Wilt Chamberlain boasted of his sexual conquest of thousands of women, and several black athletes have been in the news recently for abusing their wives. Bill Cosby, a former role model, who supposedly represented an ideal dad, has been exposed as yet another sexual predator and sentenced to prison. The black community is full of worthy black husbands and fathers that their sons should look up to. However, often young males raised by single moms do not have a father figure at hand, and they become misled by poor role models, or peer pressure drives them to join gangs or go in other more rebellious directions. They need more male role models.

Inspirational models might help to guide them by giving them new hope. In the last fifty or so years, there have been two great marches of blacks on Washington. Everyone in America is familiar with Dr. Martin Luther King's iconic 1963 "I Have a Dream" speech to 200,000 marchers gathered at the Lincoln Memorial, which many whites looked on favorably due to its pacifist, Christian nature. This March on Washington for Jobs and Freedom, led by Dr. King, emphasized the need to improve black opportunity for advancement. Regrettably, this opportunity has not been realized so far. In 1963, the black median income was about 54% of the income of whites, and by 2014, it had only improved to about 61% that of whites.

Less remembered is the 1995 Million Man March organized by the controversial Nation of Islam minister Louis Farrakhan to urge African American males to take responsibility for their own society in a Day of Atonement. This march drew several times more individuals than the 1963 march, but it never got the same attention as King's march, due to white resistance to the messenger because of Farrakhan's association with Islam, whereas King was a Christian. Yet, as controversial as Farrakhan might have been, he called for blacks to take more action and responsibility for their plight rather than relying on whites.

In his speech, Farrakhan made these remarks which emphasize creating healthy, peaceful, productive communities and avoiding drugs. Here are some key quotations from his speech:

"We talking about moving toward a perfect union. Well, pointing out fault, pointing out our wrongs is the first step. Black man, you don't have to bash white people, all we gotta do is go back home and turn our communities into productive places. All we gotta do is go back home and make our communities decent and safe place to live. And if we start dotting the Black community with businesses, opening up factories, challenging ourselves to be better than we are, White folk, instead of driving by, using the "N" word, they'll say, look, look at them. Oh, my God. They're marvelous. They're wonderful. We can't, we can't say they're inferior anymore. But, every time we drive by shoot, every time we carjack, every time we use foul, filthy language, every time we produce culturally degenerate films and tapes, putting a string in our women's backside and parading them before the world, every time we do things like this we are feeding the degenerate mind of white supremacy and I want us to stop feeding that mind and let that mind die a natural death. Take this pledge with me..... I, say your name, pledge that from this day forward I will never raise my hand with a knife or a gun to beat, cut, or shoot any member of my family or any human being, except in self-defense. I, say your name, pledge from this day forward I will never abuse my wife by striking her, disrespecting her, for she is the mother of my children and the producer of my future.....I, say your name, pledge from this day forward I will not poison my body with drugs or that which is destructive to my health and wellbeing."

At the time that Farrakhan spoke, the condition of black Americans had not improved much since Martin Luther King, and it has not improved that much since 1995. Back in 1995:

- ❖ Blacks had a poverty rate of over 40% and a median family income that was still less than 60% that of whites.

- ❖ Black unemployment was over 11%, and over 50% of teenagers over 16 were unemployed.

- ❖ Black males were being murdered at a rate nearly 8 times that of white males, and organizers believed that the government dealt with blacks with law enforcement techniques and with welfare programs that had failed the black community.

Black unemployment statistics have improved significantly by 2018 (6.5% versus 11% previously for unemployment overall, 20.8% versus 50% previously for teenagers over 16).[211] The decline since 2010 began under Obama's watch, but much of the credit must go to President Trump's economic agenda, and it really has reached historic lows. The murder rate of non-Hispanic blacks in 2016 stubbornly remained 7.9 times that of non-Hispanic whites versus 8 times that previously,[212] but in 2017, after the President took office that ratio declined to 6.3.[213] It would indeed appear that President Trump has had a more positive effect on the black community than either King or Farrakhan.

Some Conclusions and Suggestions

Thus, Farrakhan's 1995 message did not achieve its intended goal of producing a more peaceful, productive black community, just as MLK's dream had failed. Nevertheless, if black males took more responsibility for their own situation and eschewed other temptations, such as participating in an underground economy and taking drugs, the black community would be much better off.

Accordingly, I suggest that future marches with a more Christian bent or other events around the country might be organized to encourage more individual black personal responsibility, and these could be led by black role models such as Colin Powell or President Obama. In addition, middle class blacks who have moved out of urban ghettos should be encouraged to help out their less fortunate brothers, the impoverished denizens of the communities they grew up in, again by serving as role models, big brothers or the like.

Marches and nonviolent protests alone are no more likely to improve the situation now than they did previously. More sustained grassroots community organizing and interfaith partnerships to promote greater understanding and cooperation between the races may hold more promise. The inspirational work of Pope Francis on behalf of the poor hopefully will encourage more churches to aid the poor of all races and ethnicities. One problem badly in need of addressing is the poor church attendance of young African-American males.

While black women do not contribute as much to crime, they do contribute to black poverty statistics. Poverty in the black community is influenced by the low proportion of dual parent households. Since 70% of black children are raised by single black moms, that guarantees a dramatically high poverty rate. The War on Poverty initiated by LBJ in the 1960's has not helped. Although it did provide a social safety net for impoverished single moms, those single moms became ensnared by the welfare system into perpetual poverty, and too few succeeded in getting work to better their existence while simultaneously raising their kids. Their daughters followed this pattern, which perpetuated the problem.

Three things might help to get these single moms out of poverty. These are:

➢ Subsidized daycare for working single moms could enable them to go to work.

➢ Black women need a good role model, such as Condoleezza Rice or Michelle Obama, to encourage them to avoid the pitfalls of becoming single moms.

➢ Contraceptive implants, which are safe, effective, readily removable and last several years, could be used to reduce the rate of unwanted pregnancies for teenagers of all races.

PART IV: THE OPIOID CRISIS AND THE WAR ON DRUGS

- Opioids and Other Drugs

CHAPTER 7: OPIOIDS AND OTHER DRUGS

Incarceration too often has been associated with drug use. More recently, drug use has been associated with an epidemic of ever more virulent drug addiction and drug overdoses that have plagued communities of all races and ethnicities nationwide.

The High Cost of Drugs to Victims and the Economy[214]

Before considering the remedies for drug addiction and the punishments for drug dealing, let's look at the stats showing the high costs for both drug victims and the economy. While liberals may propose just getting rid of the war on drugs and taxing drugs, they fail to look at the other side of the equation which involves holding the dealers complicit in the death of millions of victims of overdoses and addiction. They also ignore the high costs due to the many repercussions of drug use, including medical expenses, damages, and property losses from crimes committed by addicts to get money for drugs, and lost productivity.

So now let's consider these ravages to society and the economy:

❖ Over 50,000 Americans died of drug overdoses in 2015, over 33,000 from using opioids. Total drug overdoses soared to over 64,000 in 2016.[215] While opioids are legal when prescribed by a physician for a patient suffering from a serious illness or injury, the vast majority of victims have abused these drugs or obtained them illegally.[216]

❖ The opioid crisis costs the U.S. economy $504 billion, according to a report from the Council of Economic Advisers, an agency under the Executive Office of the President.[217] This includes the cost of treating overdoses, abuse, lost productivity, and costs incurred by the criminal justice system from the police, prosecutors, judges, and others involved in finding and arresting those involved in drugs, processing these cases and incarcerating those convicted.

❖ Aside from the financial costs, other costs include the spread of HIV/AIDS and Hepatitis C, deaths from overdose, effects on unborn children, crime, unemployment, domestic abuse, divorce, and homelessness.[218]

❖ Heroin use is increasing, so that 600,000 people use it regularly.

❖ Nearly 40% of drug overdoses occur for those between the ages of 30 and 39. Because so many died young, in the past two years this has resulted tragically in the first decline in life expectancy in the U.S. African Americans and males have higher rates of drug overdoses than others.[219]

❖ Data obtained from health agencies shows the ravages of the drug overdose epidemic, which is estimated to be even worse in 2017 than in 2016. Drug overdoses have become the leading cause of death among Americans under 50.[220]

❖ The opioid addiction crisis has become even more deadly as a result of an increase in illicitly manufactured fentanyl and similar drugs which are *extremely* potent. Most of the time, fentanyl is sold on the street as heroin, or drug traffickers use it to make inexpensive counterfeit prescription opioids.

❖ Because of the strength of fentanyl and its derivatives, the overdoses can be so severe, according to first responders, that giving victims multiple doses of naloxone, the anti-overdose medication sometimes called Narcan, doesn't work well anymore. Sometimes responders dose overdose victims with 12 to 14 or more hits of Narcan with no effect.[221]

❖ Currently, over 2 million Americans are at risk of dying from an overdose or addiction, since many of these users are estimated to be dependent on opioids, including heroin. These Americans come from all walks of life. For instance, in Deerfield Township near Akron, Ohio, the Narcotics Anonymous meetings include lawyers, accountants, and young adults and teenagers from middle-class parents.[222]

In short, the drug crisis in America is very real, with millions of victims, including hundreds of thousands of deaths, and billions of dollars in costs. Those who are producing and selling these drugs are the main perpetrators of this crisis. Drug dealers are not just responsible for the victims of overdoses or addictions, and the huge illicit profits from drug sales, but also for the high criminal justice costs in dealing with these cases, depending on how high up you go on the drug sales chain.

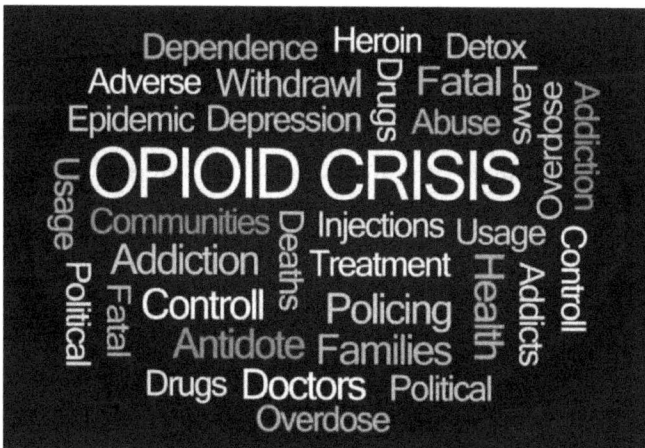

Under the circumstances, what can we do to deal with this problem? How can we penalize the dealers to cut down on the overdoses and addiction? Should the death penalty be considered for the biggest drug dealers? That's what I'll address in the following section.

Considering the Death Penalty to Solve Our National Opioid Crisis[223]

Today America is suffering from a drug crisis that has claimed hundreds of thousands of lives, affected millions more, and cost the economy many billions for the costs of interception, incarceration, medical treatment, and lost wages. The worst of the problem is due to opioids, including prescription pain killers, heroin, and synthetic derivatives of fentanyl.

The huge number of deaths due to drugs, as well as the high costs to the economy, certainly indicate the need to take action, including increased penalties. The President has even recently proposed the death penalty for dealing large quantities of drugs. Liberals are outraged by this proposal, but the President rightly points out that individual drug dealers are responsible for hundreds of overdose deaths, and we routinely demand the death penalty for mass homicides. The death penalty might well be a fit punishment, and possibly even a deterrent for future drug barons.

In determining when and how to impose the death penalty, there may be much we can learn from other countries that have used this penalty for severe drug crimes, so that's what I'll discuss next.

Countries Using the Death Penalty for Drug Dealers[224]

The Death Penalty in Singapore

Singapore has had capital punishment since its days as a British colony, and this is one reason that Singapore prides itself as being a very safe country in which to live.

At one time, Singapore had the second-highest per-capita execution rate in the world -- from 1994 to 1998. In a survey taken in 2005, 95% of the population of Singapore believed in keeping the death penalty. Singapore uses hanging to carry out its executions.

Singapore is particularly harsh on prisoners in drug cases in that 70% of the hangings have been for drug-related offenses. Under the penal code, just taking drugs into Singapore merits the death penalty, so this offense is right up there with various violent and very serious crimes, including waging or attempting to wage war against the government, piracy that endangers life, murder, kidnapping, and robbery by five or more people that results in a death. In particular, under Schedule 2 of the Misuse of Drugs Act, this mandatory death sentence applies to anyone importing, exporting, or found in possession of more than the following:

- 1200 grams of opium and containing more than 30 grams of morphine
- 30 grams of morphine
- 15 grams of diamorphine (heroin)
- 30 grams of cocaine
- 500 grams of cannabis or 1000 grams of a cannabis mixture
- 250 grams of methamphetamine.

Plus there is a sentence for anyone manufacturing certain types of drugs including:
- morphine
- diamorphine (heroin)

- cocaine

- methamphetamine

It is also presumed, under the law, that any person with a controlled drug in his or her possession knows the nature of the drug.

These death penalty provisions seem to have been effective, in that according to some reports, Singapore has one of the lowest prevalence of drug abuse around the world. For instance, one blogger Benjamin Chang, reports that in over 20 years, the number of drug abusers arrested each year has declined from over 6000 in the early 1990s to about 2000 in 2011. There has also been a decline in the number executed for drug related crimes from the period when these executions were at a peak from 1994 to 2001, averaging about 20 to 40 executions a year. They dropped from zero to three each year during the period from 2007 to 2017.[225]

The government and its citizens believe that the policy has helped to keep Singaporeans safe. In the government view, the death penalty is only used in the most serious of crimes, including drug offenses, which sends a strong message of deterrence to potential offenders. As stated by the Ministry of Home Affairs in January 2004 -- a position reaffirmed by the continuation of Singapore's death penalty policies: "The application of the death penalty is only reserved for 'very serious crimes... (the) death penalty has been effective in keeping Singapore one of the safest places in the world to work and live in." More recently, a similar statement about the effectiveness of the death penalty has been asserted by Vivian Balakrisknan, the Minister of Foreign Affairs, in a speech to the UN in September 2016. As she asserted: "In our view, capital punishment for drug-related offenses and for murder has been a key element in keeping Singapore drug free and keeping Singapore safe."[226]

Additionally, the success of combating drug abuse with the death penalty has inspired some American elected officials and office-seekers since 2012 to urge applying the Singaporean model in the U.S. For example, Michael Bloomberg, former Mayor of

New York City, said that the U.S. could learn from nations like Singapore's approach to drug trafficking in that "executing a handful of people saves thousands and thousands of lives." And high-profile Republican Newt Gingrich has long advocated bringing Singaporean methods to support the U.S. War on Drugs.

How China Is Using the Death Penalty for Drug Dealers

Like Singapore, China has had a long history of capital punishment as a legal penalty for murder and drug trafficking.

China had an enormous opium addiction problem that had been inflicted on them by the British importing opium from India throughout the 19th century to both make profits and pacify the population. Two opium wars took place in this century, and the British prevailed, even gaining Hong Kong as a result of one of the wars. By 1906, there were 13.5 million opium addicts in China out of a total population of 400 million. Those 13.5 million addicts represented 27% of the adult male population. Now due to their crackdown on drugs, China has considerably reduced its opium problem.

A major reason for the death penalty is to dissuade drug trafficking, and the public nature of these executions shows China's commitment to this policy, which has gained widespread public support. For example, in December 2017, thousands of observers watched as 10 people were sentenced to death in a sports stadium in Lufeng in the southern Guangdong providence, about 100 miles from Hong Kong. Of the 10 executed, seven were convicted of drug-related crimes, while the other prisoners were found guilty of murder and robbery.[227]

To put on this spectacle, local residents received an official notice through the social media inviting them to attend the sentencing. As the crowd watched, a police truck with its blaring sirens arrived with the accused, who were each surrounded by four officers wearing sunglasses. Then, one by one, the accused were escorted to a small platform to hear their sentences read. After that, they were whisked away to be executed. Such open air sentencing is staged as part of China's drug crackdown, where drug dealers are treated much like terrorists.

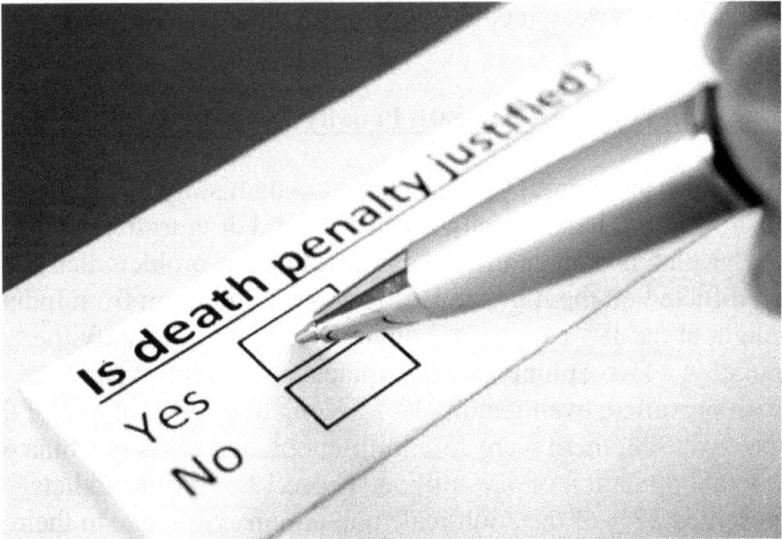

The Case Against the Death Penalty as a Fix for Our Drug Problems[228]

Since imposing the death penalty for drug traffickers has worked so well in Singapore and China, the next consideration is whether a similar measure would work here. It seems it might, since the U.S. already applies the death penalty on many crimes, including murder, terrorism, and treason.

In many ways, our society is not like those in Singapore or China. To be effective, China uses public sentencing to strengthen the deterrent. That might not go over as well in the U.S. Singapore has used extensive top-down authority to keep its many ethnic groups in check and to guard against offenses to the public order, even gum chewing, which are the kinds of things that states' rights groups in the U.S. would find offensive. But the biggest cultural difference is that Asian societies value their elders more than we do and are more willing to do as they are told. Besides, U.S. liberals are not inclined to defer to the President on matters where they disagree.

These Asian countries probably don't have as many violent foreign drug traffickers as we do. Given the lucrative profits inherent in the drug trade, it is hard to imagine drug kingpins and gangs in Mexico, Central America and Colombia being deterred by the threat of a death penalty. In fact, these gangs are known for violence, which has resulted in tens of thousands of deaths in these turf battles. And some cartel leaders have been able to hide away for years to rule their gangs, and a few have managed to live like kings in their "prisons" or have gotten accomplices outside to help them engineer elaborate escapes, such as El Chapo did as one of the biggest Mexican drug lords.

What else would need to be taken into consideration? Here are some slippery slope issues:

- Where do you draw the line? Should the death penalty be imposed on those who have sold X number of grams of heroin in a certain period of time or those who have supplied the heroin that resulted in Y number of cases of heroin overdose? And how would these numbers be determined? Whatever numbers are set for the penalties to kick in would have to be substantiated in a court of law. How would we translate grams of heroin to milligrams of fentanyl? Would a small time dealer who had been given a bad batch of fentanyl-laced "heroin" be more liable than the bigger dealer who supplied him? If he had checked out the product personally, he'd probably be dead. Many lower level dealers or smugglers act more as conduits or "mules" who sell or transport what they have been given without checking the merchandise. How guilty should they be, given their lack of knowledge of the potency or value of what they are transporting?

- What about prescription painkillers? There is little doubt these started our national crisis, since opioids were responsible for 42,249 deaths in 2016 according to the Center for Disease Control and Prevention, [229] and 63,600 deaths that year according to the National Center for Health Statistics. [230] So it's no wonder that there is a sense of crisis about these drugs leading to a major cause of death. Yet relatively few deaths result directly from unintentional overdoses of prescription painkillers. We are certainly right to limit their use, but it seems excessive to impose the death penalty for prescribing physicians or the companies that manufacture them, since these drugs have their legal uses and save millions from debilitating pain or death. Shouldn't the real culprits be the drug dealers who provide these pills through illicit channels to users and abusers?

- What about other illegal drugs? Methamphetamine might well fall into the same category of causing deaths, although not as many (only 7663 in 2016, according to the "Overdose Death Rates" report from the National Institute for Drug Abuse).[231] Personally, I would contend it should be in the same category as the opioids. But what about PCP or ecstasy? These may cause violent behavior but probably not as many deaths. What about cocaine? Overdoses due to cocaine totaled 10,619 in 2016. [232]   Crack cocaine devastated the black community some number of years ago, then subsided, but overdoses due to cocaine are on the rise again more recently.[233]

- What about marijuana? There are very few reported cases of death by marijuana overdose. It is not even as dangerous to adults as alcohol. And now marijuana is legal medicinally in 31 states, and recreationally in 9 of those. The President recently even assured Colorado Senator Cory Gardner that he would consider marijuana usage a states' rights issue rather than a federal one, which would protect marijuana usage where it has been legalized.[234] A majority of Americans (61-64%, including 51% of Republicans according to polls by the Pew Research Center and *Forbes*)[235] favor its legalization. Under the circumstances, it would be hard to imagine making the death penalty applicable to marijuana dealers.

- What about alcohol? We've been there before with Prohibition. Too bad that didn't work, because alcohol probably costs even more to society than the opioid crisis, including lots of violence and deaths. The President knows this all too well, having lost his brother to alcohol addiction. Wisely, he just says no, but most Americans don't seem to be able to follow suit. The death penalty won't work for alcohol. There are too many millions of users.

- What about tobacco? It causes even more deaths than alcohol. The deaths are much more delayed and chronic and have cost the health of sufferers and the healthcare system a fortune. Unfortunately tobacco is still legal; otherwise cigarette manufacturing executives who deceived the public for years would be prime candidates for death penalty consideration.

As you can see, there are numerous practical considerations that would make the death penalty idea problematic to implement. The President deserves credit for politically incorrect outside-the-box thinking on this critical issue, and I agree that many opioid traffickers deserve the death penalty, but I am afraid that a greater emphasis on the other aspects of his proposed fixes for the opioid crisis is probably in order. Thus, I want to propose the following suggestions for overcoming this crisis.

Some Suggestions for Dealing with the Opioid Crisis[236]

I have discussed the President's suggestion that the death penalty should be imposed on drug traffickers, why it is justified, and yet how its implementation would create severe practical difficulties. If not this approach, what other strategies should be pursued? Alas, there is no one simple fix, so several different strategies need to be pursued simultaneously.

1. The President recommended mandatory minimum sentencing as a penalty for distributing certain opioids, with sentencing duration dictated by the amount of substance seized. This crackdown may help reduce supply, but it will need to be supplemented with greater interdiction efforts at all ports of entry and along our borders. Another reason for greater border security!

2. The President also recommended expanding access to *proven* treatment and recovery efforts. This recommendation is primarily aimed at reducing demand

rather than supply. There are many treatment centers and plans, some more effective than others. Once the best strategies are determined, such treatments should be carried out on a mandatory basis on addicts in prisons and jails, even if that requires segregated facilities for them. Otherwise, they will easily relapse once released and revert back to a life of crime to feed their habit. Different treatment plans could be tried out on prison populations in order to determine which are the most effective. Sentences could be reduced for those who "come clean," by both stopping use and identifying their own suppliers.

3. Finally, the President recommended broadening awareness and education of the crisis. By now it is likely that most adult Americans are familiar with the crisis, which suggests that adolescent youth and their parents should be targeted. An educational campaign in all schools, including a series of videos about the dangers of addiction, deaths due to drugs, and the crackdown on drug dealers, might help reduce the influence of adolescent peer pressure. Videos should also be produced for parents advising them what to be on the lookout for and giving them advice on dealing with their adolescent children on this issue.

Although all three of these sets of recommendations in the President's plan have been proposed previously and represent more conventional approaches than the death penalty, they are all worthwhile, and the President must be complimented on putting them forth and implementing them with actual spending. Kudos to the President.

Following are two suggestions of mine for dealing with the crisis:

1. Set up a tip line for information that leads to the arrest of drug traffickers. This tip line can be set up so that callers can protect their anonymity, as well as claim substantial rewards by

providing information that leads to the arrest of high-level drug dealers who are subject to the death penalty. These rewards can be tiered, so that those who target higher-level drug dealers can earn more, and an encrypted system can be set up so that tipsters can both remain anonymous yet claim a reward.

2. Provide more funds for research into better addiction treatments. As mentioned previously, the President wishes to increase access to *proven* treatment programs. Present treatments are only moderately effective and relapse occurs frequently. More effective treatments are sorely needed. The opioid epidemic is every bit as critical as the HIV/AIDS epidemic was, and yet addiction research receives only a fraction of the funds that AIDS research did. Opioid users are not able to mount the kind of concerted lobbying effort that homosexuals managed, because they are debilitated by their addiction, and the families of opioid users have not been able to lobby for them either, since often addicts are estranged from their families. Thus, providing assistance with researching treatment options is one arena where the federal government has to intervene.[237]

These recommendations are needed because we have been losing the war on drugs. How badly and at what cost? I'll describe this struggle in the next section.

The Deleterious Effects of the War on Drugs[238]

The drug war is not being won. The drug war is taking money from budgets that could be better spent elsewhere. There are perverse incentives in the system to keep this costly war going. For example, the officer who makes drug arrests gets overtime for doing the paperwork for each arrest. As a result, he can make many more arrests than an investigator who spends more time solving a homicide case. Thus, the cop who pursues the drug arrests is the one who gets promoted.[4]

The drug war is also very expensive due to the cost of imprisoning those who are convicted. Incarceration alone is very expensive. In 2010, it cost between $14,603 and $60,076 per year, depending on the state.[239] To these costs must be added the costs of arresting them and processing them from their arrest to conviction.

Reforming the government's drug policies could have positive economic benefits, since many of those imprisoned were arrested for drug offenses. Yet the war on drugs has failed to stop drug use or the spread of international gangs. Instead, the underground nature of the drug industry has led to a large criminal element involved in producing, distributing, and selling drugs. In turn, that has not only drawn gangs in the U.S., Mexico, and other countries into providing illegal drugs for U.S. customers, but it has resulted in increased costs for law enforcement, the courts, and corrections for processing drug dealers and users through the system.

As former Senator Jim Webb has pointed out, "A dangerous form of organized and sometimes deadly gang activity has infiltrated America's towns and cities. It comes largely from our country's southern border, and much of the criminal activity centers around the movement of illegal drugs."[240] Much of this criminal activity comes from Mexican drug cartels, as they engage in extremely brutal actions to spread their profitable business enterprises through our cities.

Thus, one approach has traditionally been to try to curtail the import and sale of these drugs, an approach advocated by the Trump administration in securing our southern border. Yet, as long as there has been high demand, the drug sellers have found multiple channels for bringing drugs to the end-user customer, which has meant the prohibition approach has not been effective, while costing astronomical amounts of money.

Educating kids and adults against using drugs has not fixed the problem either, given peer pressure and how good the drugs make the users feel at first. Before they realize it, they become addicted.

The medical profession has contributed to this problem by overprescribing opiates for pain. At present we have a clear opioid addiction epidemic that everyone agrees has reached crisis proportions, both in rural as well as urban areas. Many more treatment centers must be opened to treat these addicts rather than merely incarcerating them.

On the other hand, the American public is growing ever more in favor of a permissive attitude toward marijuana. Marijuana may well be less harmful than alcohol, and our prison and jail costs could go down considerably if marijuana possession were decriminalized to a level similar to a speeding ticket. Some states have even voted in favor of legalization and taxation, particularly since traditional approaches have proved very costly and aren't working. Marijuana represents an unusual issue where states' rights advocates are now advocating permissiveness, while the federal government is resisting. In addition, younger adults without children are generally in favor of less restriction of marijuana use, while parents of children have legitimate concerns. Medical marijuana appears to represent a first step in the direction of approval of recreational marijuana in many states. If the federal government fails to clamp down on marijuana use, the experience of those states which have approved its use should be carefully monitored, particularly for its effects on marijuana use by under-age adolescents, whose brain development might be adversely affected.

Drug Overdoses vs. Homicides[241]

For all the concerns about the numbers of gun-related homicides, an even bigger villain is the use of opioids, which causes more deaths by overdose than death by guns.

There are approximately 8600 gun homicides per year. Opioid overdose deaths are about three times higher. The numbers become similar only if one adds in the 22,000 annual suicides involving firearms, although most of the opioid overdoses were accidental, not done with any suicidal intent. Thus, even though both problems are difficult to deal with, reducing opioid addiction should be a priority, along with taking steps to reduce the number of homicides.

In the November 4, 2016 issue of *Science* magazine, in an article "Pot and Pain", Greg Miller indicated that the epidemic of opioid overdose deaths has been increasing. In 2014 alone, 28,647 opioid overdose deaths were reported, 18,073 of them from prescription opioids, and reportedly, the numbers have increased since then. This serious problem was even raised as an issue in several states during the 2016 Presidential campaign.

In his article, Miller pointed out that cannabis might be used as a painkiller alternative to opioids. The opioid death rate makes opioids a much more dangerous class of drugs than pot. After the most recent election, medical marijuana is currently legal in 31 states plus the District of Columbia, and its recreational use is now legal in 9 states and D.C. Pot is also not as serious a health hazard as alcohol, which at 88,000 deaths a year accounts for over three times as many deaths annually than opioids.

Nevertheless, marijuana use is still illegal federally and continues to be considered a gateway to other drugs of abuse. The Obama administration did not seek to challenge marijuana use in states that have approved its use, while President Trump abstains from alcohol and all drugs that are considered addictive, but he has said he believes legalization of marijuana should be left up to the states. However, his selection for Attorney General, Senator Jeff Sessions, is a vocal opponent of marijuana legalization. Rudy Giuliani is known to be a fervent believer in the War on Drugs, even though it has been very unsuccessful. It is therefore unclear whether a Trump administration will consider permitting federal marijuana use for pain as a means of combating the opioid epidemic.

Ideally, marijuana should be decriminalized, primarily to reduce the huge numbers of individuals unnecessarily incarcerated for marijuana possession. The possibility that marijuana could help cut down on the scourge of opioid overdoses represents a new argument in favor of its medical use.

An irony in this debate is that the states' rights advocates are the liberal/progressives, in that 19 of the 31 states which have legalized medical marijuana voted against President Trump, as did 8 of the 9 states which legalized recreational pot. On most issues, usually the conservatives are the states' rights advocates, while liberals/progressives generally favor federal rights.

Prescription: Establish More Drug Treatment and More Drug Courts[242]

The cost of fighting drugs over the last 40 years has been in the trillions. We are on track to spend 40 billion dollars in the war on drugs this year alone.[243] Even though the U.S. has devoted many resources to drug interdiction, this prohibition approach has not worked. More than 22 million Americans use illegal drugs as of this writing, and for most addicts, predatory crime — larceny, shoplifting, sneak thievery, burglary, embezzlement, robbery, and so forth — is a necessary way of life in order to support oneself and one's addiction. Drug addiction makes it difficult to maintain a job, and addicts often turn to crime to get the monies for food, shelter, and to obtain the drugs they "need" lest they suffer debilitating withdrawal symptoms.[244]

Aside from addictions to cocaine, amphetamines, and other controlled drugs, opiate addiction, once restricted to urban minority communities, has reached epidemic proportions throughout the heartland. It was even a bipartisan issue in the 2016 presidential campaign. Physicians overprescribing pain medications for illnesses and injuries may have been responsible for turning once responsible, respectable patients to addiction. Then, once hooked, these patients become slaves to their craving. In part because of this genesis of addiction, physicians and scientists commonly agree that addiction is better viewed as an illness than as a moral failing.

Unfortunately, once in the grips of an addiction, individuals can remain stuck, since very few of those affected can afford the kind of treatment center that cured Rush Limbaugh or other high-profile celebrities. Even many middle and upper income addicts don't have the kinds of funds to join these expensive "kick-the-addiction" programs. So this is a widespread problem that affects all classes in society; it is no longer confined to the inner cities, and it's time to shed its gangster image, because addiction affects us all.

Thus, it's time to change our approach to those who use illegal drugs by offering drug treatment plans rather than punishment. From a cost-savings standpoint, drug treatment reduces expenditures. These big financial savings to society result from less "violent and property crimes, prison expenses, court and criminal costs, emergency room visits, child abuse and neglect, lost child support, foster care and welfare costs, reduced productivity, unemployment, and victimization."[245]

Moreover, according to the National Institute of Drug Abuse (NIDA), drug treatment can "cut drug abuse in half, reduce criminal activity up to 80%, and reduce arrests up to 64%."[246] From a healthcare perspective, the spread of HIV/AIDS, hepatitis, and other infectious diseases is decreased, as such diseases are often passed on by drug addicts sharing needles.

Extensive research has shown that treatment for abusers in the criminal justice system as well as for those living outside it has proven effective. As the National Institute of Drug Abuse (NIDA) notes: "Treatment is an effective intervention for drug abusers... Longitudinal outcome studies find that those who participate in community-based drug abuse treatment programs commit fewer crimes than those who do not."[247]

Accordingly, we should establish a new drug treatment approach for those in the criminal justice system. Here's how we can successfully implement it:

➤ Encourage sentencing changes to allow some nonviolent drug offenders to get out of prison early, if they complete an intensive treatment program.

➤ Instead of sentencing non-violent drug offenders to prison, judges should find less restrictive penalties, such as time served, coupled with treatment and probation or community service.

➤ Incorporate drug abuse treatment programs into a variety of criminal justice settings. These programs might include treatment as a condition of probation and drug courts that combine judicial monitoring and sanctions with treatment, in-prison. Then the ex-con might participate in community-based treatment after being discharged or while still being supervised under parole or probation.[248]

➤ Mainstream the use of drug courts for nonviolent offenders, an approach that has worked around the country. It has offered addicts an opportunity to participate in a treatment program, along with help in finding work if they are successful in completing the program. The quarter of offenders who graduate from these drug courts have greatly reduced rates of recidivism and re-arrest rates, and these programs cost our cities and states significantly less than standard prison sentences.[249,250,251,252]

➤ Extend cost-effective programs that work to the public at large in less restrictive settings.

➤ As a last resort, consider the Portuguese approach of monitoring drug addicts and providing them with free methadone. Compared to 312 deaths per million from drug-related deaths in the U.S., Portugal has only 6 per million. This doesn't solve the drug problem, but it does reduce its horrific consequences. The cost of such treatment is a tiny fraction of the cost of what we continue to spend on the War on Drugs.[253]

Prescription: End the War on Marijuana to Reduce Violence and Possibly Bring Revenue to Cash-Starved States and Cities[254]

Business writers in conservative business publications, such as *Forbes*, have strongly advocated ending the drug wars, and at the very least, decriminalizing marijuana. In fact, in addition to the 9 states and Washington, D.C. which have legalized recreational marijuana, an additional 13 states have decriminalized possession of small amounts of marijuana without legalizing its recreational use.[255]

Decriminalization would have a significant economic benefit. Out of the drug arrests made back in 2009, more than half (858,408) were for cannabis violations — with about 89% of those arrests for possession only— and we are on pace to reach 780,000 cannabis arrests this year.[256] Fortunately, far fewer are actually incarcerated for cannabis. Estimates range from 10,000-20,000 for those in prison for marijuana possession only.[257] At an average of $30,000 per prisoner we spend $300-600 million on cannabis incarcerations for cannabis possession, and we spend untold more for processing the additional three quarters of a million people annually arrested for cannabis possession.

As of this writing, more than 50% of the U.S. population supports legalizing pot, and a growing number of states and cities have passed laws that make it legal to grow and distribute medical marijuana. One of the latest states to allow the recreational use of marijuana is Alaska, long a conservative bastion in the United States. So if Alaska can opt to legalize the recreational use of pot, why can't other states?

Well, Attorney General Sessions is opposed. As stated previously, this is one issue where conservatives may favor a federal approach, while liberals advocate for state rights.

Business investors have made the case that if marijuana in all forms was legalized, it could be taxed by federal, state, and city governments, and provide significant revenue, particularly for cash-starved states and cities.

How and why should we handle the possibility of legalizing marijuana? Some possible ways include:

> Decriminalize the possession of small quantities of recreational marijuana so it is considered only an infraction, such as a citation or speeding ticket, in certain test states and observe the results. If the negative consequences of decriminalization are small, more states will decriminalize it.

> Observe closely what happens in those states that have legalized medical marijuana, and then take steps to legalize medical marijuana elsewhere if prudent.

> Observe the results obtained in states that have legalized and taxed all marijuana. If the results show minimal adverse consequences, allow more states to legalize recreational marijuana and invest the money that is now going toward interdiction and prison building back to government coffers, along with the income from state marijuana taxes. If marijuana is legalized, it should be done in a responsible manner. Washington State's policy seems a sound one to adopt, since it includes these provisions:

1. Provide "accountable oversight by an agency of government:" A state agency should write regulations regarding the growing, producing, and selling of marijuana. These regulations should include tight

limitations on advertising and the prevention of access to pot by minors. The agency should have the authority to issue licenses to growers, producers, and sellers and to enforce adherence to the rules.

2. Include a well-funded marijuana education program based on science rather than ideology.

3. Have a well-funded prevention program to help young people use marijuana wisely and avoid abusing it.

4. Establish a treatment program for marijuana dependence.

5. Require an evaluation of the new model's impact.

6. Make state funds available for research on marijuana by the state's two major research universities.[258]

How the Opioid Crisis Is Affecting the Divisions in America

The opioid crisis and the debate over the appropriate punishment for drug dealers both reflect the great divides between different groups in America, as discussed in the next chapter. Here I want to point up the divisions affected by these two issues.

First, different groups have widely divergent views on how to deal with the opioid crisis. On the one side, liberals and those on the Coast preferred more protective policies to treat the opioid abuser and lesser penalties, including treatment, for sellers of drugs. As one example of this more support the abuser approach, San Francisco and Gavin Newsome, the lead candidate for governor, have thrown their support behind centers where drug addicts can go to get their drugs. By contrast, conservatives and those in Middle America and the South tend to advocate a no drugs policy that includes a crackdown on drugs and harsh penalties for dealers, with the President advocating the death penalty for the biggest dealers. They definitely don't want any treatment centers dispensing any kind of drug, since they want to stop drug use, not promote a safe space to obtain drugs. By contrast, the liberals and Coast dwellers tend to oppose the death penalty for anyone, not only the top drug dealers

However, the opioid crisis is so severe that even these political differences could be overcome. Most recently a bipartisan bill on the opioid crisis cleared the Senate by a 98-1 margin[259] and will be signed by the President. The nation cannot wait for other problems to reach similar crisis proportions before taking political action.

The political divisions mentioned here are just the tip of the iceberg when it comes to the divisions between many different types of groups. The divisions have to be understood and then bridged if we are to make meaningful progress on any other issue. That's what I'll discuss next.

PART V: HEALING THE DIVISIONS IN U.S. SOCIETY

- **Understanding Our Divisions**

CHAPTER 8: UNDERSTANDING OUR DIVISIONS

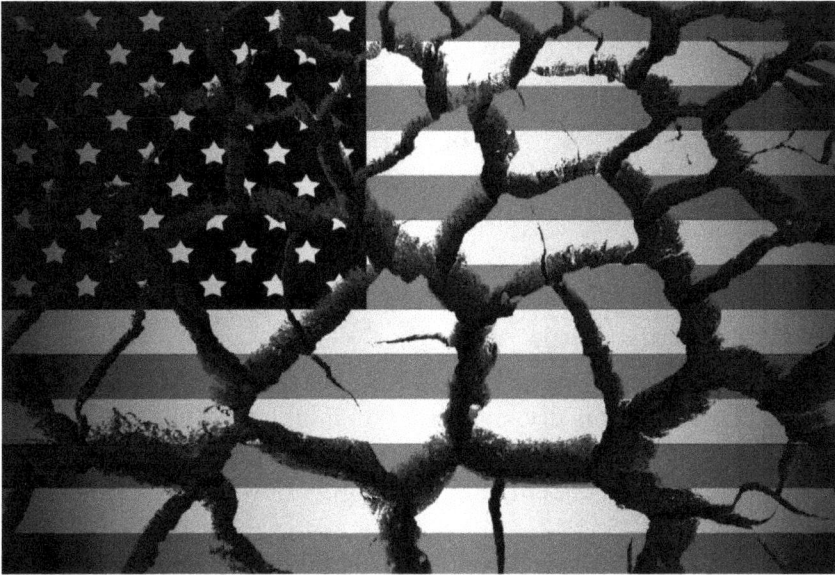

Why the United States is So Divided and How it Can Be Put Back Together Again[260]

We have to face some grim truths today, or our great nation could easily erupt in flames. The Civil War never really ended. Blacks and whites never really succeeded in mending fences. The North-South divide continues to this date and is further complicated by the divide involving Hispanics, divides between the Coasts and the Heartland (Mid-West, South and Rust Belt). Another division is between rural and urban America. And today the hostility is greater than ever in the party battles between Republicans and Democrats. In addition to these geopolitical divides, there are generational and financial divides that threaten the country.

To see all this divisiveness, you might conclude that the U.S. is clearly done for. Yet, all partisans on both sides of these divides are interdependent, and that might allow for a gleam of hope.

I'll describe how this divisiveness developed and discuss in more detail the nature of these divides. Then I'll suggest some possible solutions to help bring us back together.

<u>The Racial Divide: Origins</u>[261]

This country was born of slaveholders. The father of the country, George Washington, and many who signed the Declaration of Independence and the Constitution were slaveholders.

Although slaves were treated very badly, they were very valuable. They were considered property -- valuable property. In 1860 each slave cost an average of at least $20,000 in today's dollars. But a lot of wealthy families in the South could afford them: 31% of families in the Confederacy owned slaves, and slaves made up 38% of the South's population.

The entire economy of the South depended on slaves. Their states' rights were being threatened, which led to the inevitable march toward a Civil War less than 100 years after the birth of the country.[262]

The 1860 election of Abraham Lincoln with only 40% of the popular vote in a three person race hastened the onset of the war, and this war was truly horrendous. It accounted for over 600,000 deaths -- as many deaths as all other United States wars combined. And the country still is traumatized by it, particularly the South, as reflected in the support for the Confederacy and its symbols in many communities throughout the South.

Could the Civil War have been avoided? Probably only by allowing the South to secede, which the North was loath to do. But suppose the South had seceded without challenge from the North. Would slavery still be permitted today? It's not likely, because slavery is not acceptable anywhere anymore. That means that if the South had won and continued to base its economy on the labor of slaves, at some point the South would have had to reform its entire economic system, as well as overcome its resentment about all the freed slaves left living there. It would have made the blacks the scapegoats for all the economic upheavals it experienced, just as it scapegoated them after the Civil War.

BRITISH NORTH AMERICA

Washington Territory

Oregon

Dakota Territory

Minn.

Wis.

Mich.

Maine

Vt.

N.H.

N.Y.

Mass.

Conn.

R.I.

Nevada Terr.

Utah Territory

Colorado Territory

Nebraska Territory

Iowa

United States of America

Penn.

N.J.

California

Pacific Ocean

New Mexico Territory

Kansas

Mo.

Ill.

Ind.

Ohio

W. Va. (1863)

Ky.

Va.

Del.

Md.

Indian Territory

Ark.

Tenn.

N.C.

S.C.

Atlantic Ocean

Miss.

Ala.

Ga.

Fort Sumter
April 12-14, 1861

Confederate States of America

Union and Confederate boundary

Free state

Territory

Slave state

Texas

La.

MEXICO

Florida

Gulf of Mexico

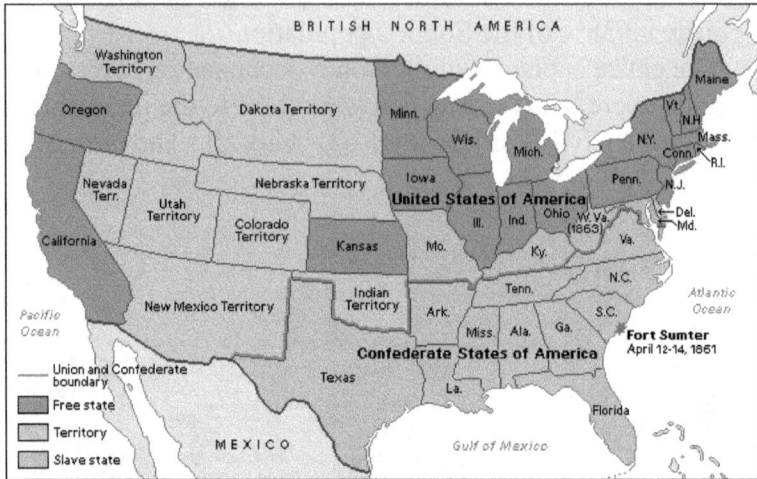

Could the Civil War have been terminated earlier? Yes, if Lee had been less reckless at Gettysburg in 1863 by ordering Pickett's charge, losing the battle. Or if Hood had been less reckless in the summer of 1864 attacking Sherman around Atlanta, hastening its fall, Lincoln would probably have lost the 1864 election and some sort of truce would have been declared. Still, at some point the South would have had to give up its slaves, and the same white resentment of blacks would have surfaced.

But the Civil War DID make that resentment far worse. The South was razed by Sherman's march to the sea. It was completely defeated and had to surrender.

.

Attitude of Southern Whites toward Blacks

After the war, the South was humiliated and then subjected to profiteering by Northern carpetbaggers. It couldn't even count on its slaves to rebuild. Before the war, the blacks had been considered valuable property, and now that they were rendered free by government fiat, Southerners not only lost the war, but many of them lost their most valuable property.

As a result, the South blamed not only the North but the slaves for its devastation in the aftermath of war. Worse yet, Southerners still had to live with the former slaves. No wonder the whites hated them.

The Southerners feared the now free blacks, too. After all, they feared that former slaves might want to get their revenge for all those years of mistreatment. Moreover, they fervently believed that white women had to be protected from black males, lest their women be ravished by these former slaves and their progeny.

Given this deep animosity of blacks by the Southerners, for many years the Jim Crow system in the South ensured that blacks were kept in their place. In response, many former slaves migrated to the North in hopes of escaping their plight in the South. Since new job opportunities were concentrated in Northern cities, that's where many of them went.

Attitudes of Northern Whites toward Blacks

Many Northerners had negative attitudes towards the former slaves who migrated north, as well. As late as 1863, President Lincoln mused about deporting slaves after they were freed.[263] Whites in the North didn't want former slaves coming to compete for their jobs. They had lost a lot of men in the fight to abolish slavery and the entire nation was financially and emotionally drained. They felt blacks already owed them enough for freeing them. Why couldn't they just stay where they were and be grateful? Since the North had had few slaves, they weren't responsible for slavery. So why should they have to help the Southerners overcome what was their fault in the first place by contributing jobs or money for freed slaves?

Attitudes of Blacks toward Whites

What about black feelings? They had endured slavery for about a hundred years, including in many cases subhuman living conditions and extremely hard labor. They had experienced their families being torn apart and sold, barbaric torture, and even sometimes castration.

Many had remained loyal to their captors, perhaps out of necessity, but most resented their plight and their former masters. The Founding Fathers had written "All men are created equal", but the blacks knew they didn't count as men to the white Southerners who held the reins of power. To them, the blacks were just beasts of burden, and often they were killed if they were captured after escaping.

Then the Civil War erupted. With the exception of a very few all black units fighting for the North, blacks weren't allowed to fight on either side. They weren't wanted.

Then, suddenly, they were free---but penniless...and hated and feared by their former captors. They owned no land and were forced into sharecropping, so that now they tended the land for Southern white owners who leased it to them at exorbitant fees. They were free and their families were no longer being torn apart, but aside from that, their lot was only marginally improved over that as slaves. And they resented having been enslaved by the whites they still had to live amongst.

Summary

Whites still bear the responsibility for what they did to the blacks they enslaved. Arguably, the subjugation and enslavement of the blacks was in some ways much like what whites did to Native American Indians, who were slaughtered or marginalized on reservations. While whites directly killed the Native Americans, their policies and treatment of blacks in the inner cities has led to a high death rate due to crime, poverty and higher rates of disease than in other population groups. In effect, they continued to treat not only the first generation of freed blacks but their future generations as second class citizens – a practice that continues to today for black Americans as a whole, despite some notable success stories, primarily in sports, politics and entertainment and the emergence of a small black middle class.

This singling out and mistreatment of an entire ethnic group has included the making iconic movies like *Birth of a Nation*, where good white robed Ku Klux Klansmen defended the nation from the scourge of evil blacks. The movie was acclaimed in the North as well as the South.

Thus, whites did free the slaves, at least legally, but, once freed, they were feared. The aftermath of the Civil War might have been the appropriate time for reparations to blacks, but the country was broke, and whites felt they had done more than enough for blacks.

We can't change any of this history, but we can be more aware of what happened and try to understand how blacks and Southern whites came to the disparate attitudes they hold. Change for the better depends on that understanding, as does the desire to Make America Great Again.

This racial divide, dating back to colonial times, continues after the Civil War to today. Here's what happened since their emancipation and where things stand now.

The Racial Divide: Our Bleak Present[264]

It wasn't an easy life up North for blacks fleeing the Jim Crow South in the hundred years after the Civil War. When factories had to cut back or close, blacks suffered the most, since they were the first to lose work and quickly sink into poverty. In most U.S. cities, they also faced rampant segregation, because each ethnic group was most comfortable in its own homogeneous neighborhood. While blacks were undoubtedly most comfortable around other blacks, the neighborhoods where they lived became the poorest and most crime-ridden – with much of the crime due to impoverished conditions. Another later contributor to this concentration of poverty and crime was that the whites who could escaped to the suburbs, leaving the inner cities to the poor blacks.

Then, in 1964, a hundred years after the Civil War, President Lyndon Baines Johnson declared a War on Poverty, followed soon afterward by affirmative action programs. Both the War on Poverty and these programs were well intentioned, but they were also subject to the law of unintended consequences. The War on Poverty resulted in a welfare system which trapped many poor blacks in a subsistence existence without sufficient incentive to improve their lot.

Similarly, affirmative action provided the benefit of establishing a significant black middle class, but these blacks moved out to the suburbs, further impoverishing the black brethren they left behind in the inner cities, resulting in black ghettos. Once out of the 'hood, the middle class blacks began to relate more to their own success and that of the whites around them than to the blacks left behind in the 'hood, as happened with O.J. Simpson.

The unintended consequence was that the increasingly impoverished 'hood became rife with crime, and more and more blacks were locked up, many for petty crimes, in the "Get Tough on Crime" pushes starting in the 1980s. An enormous number of blacks were imprisoned as a result, often with long sentences of many years for relatively minor offenses like sharing some drugs with a friend. Their incarceration further decimated the 'hood and broke down families.

The prison statistics for black males are truly a national shame. As many as a third of all black men end up in prison at some point in their life, and this high rate of imprisonment has given the United States the dubious distinction of imprisoning more people than any other country in the world, based either on total numbers or on the percent of the population in prison or jail.

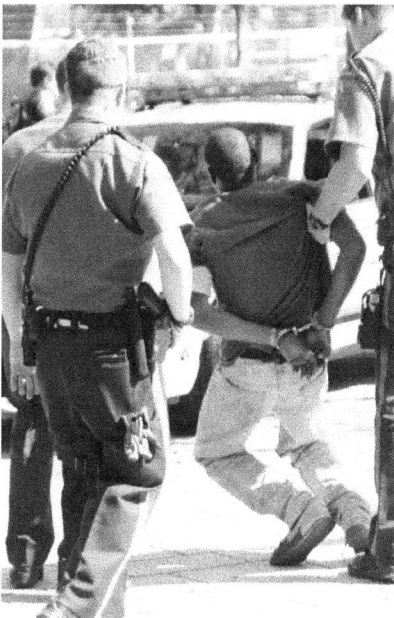

Further exacerbating the problem of black males ending up without jobs or in prison is that more than two-thirds of all blacks born are raised by single moms.[265] Since so many black males are unemployed, involved in crime, or imprisoned, young black males raised by single moms have no good male role models to guide them to living a more productive life. As a result, they drop out of school, face extremely high unemployment rates, participate in a lot of violent crime, and feel harassed by police who believe they are appropriately responding to the high rate of crime in black neighborhoods.

No wonder blacks distrust the police, and no wonder the police distrust blacks. They co-exist in a very unstable relationship which can deteriorate rapidly in response to any incident, and frequently does. Whites, who have largely abandoned downtown areas of many cities in their flight to the suburbs, would just as soon not know what goes on in the 'hood, as long as it doesn't affect them.

This mix of black-police confrontation and middle class white apathy is toxic. It is as if the middle class whites inserted the police between themselves and the blacks, creating a powder keg that can blow up at any time.

However, there may be some ways to help reduce this tension, as illustrated by two recent cases, which both used video evidence to attain a just result. Then, both sides can agree that justice has been done, so protests about injustice are not needed.

In the first case, North Carolina white police officer Michael Slager was tried for the 2015 shooting death of Walter Scott, a black American. The result was a hung jury, but Scott subsequently pled guilty to violating the Scott's civil rights by using excessive force, and he received a 20 year prison sentence in December, 2017.[266]

In the second case, a white Chicago police officer Jason Van Dyke received a second degree murder guilty verdict in 2018 for killing 17-year old black teen Laquan McDonald in 2014. Since this verdict was reached by a jury of seven whites, three Hispanics, one Asian American, and only one African American,[267] that should help to convince blacks that justice is indeed possible in a white officer - black victim situation. Unfortunately, the celebration of such a verdict by blacks can serve to politicize the situation, adding to the anger of citizens who usually support the police and thereby contributing to the divisions in American society.

Suggested Solutions[268]

Is there any solution? No one solution will suffice, but several combined together might.

> Establish more community policing. More black cops need to be recruited to help police the high crime neighborhoods where they live. All police also need to be given special training in community interaction.

> Train police to take less forceful steps to calm down a suspect in order to make an orderly arrest.

➢ To further reduce racial incidents between police and blacks, police should be screened for personality characteristics they might have in common with police who have killed innocent blacks or who have shot too quickly at suspects resisting arrest. Those personality types who are too quick to respond aggressively could be assigned to desk duties or low crime neighborhoods.

➢ Neighborhood watches should be encouraged in the black community, at least during daytime hours.

➢ Young blacks raised by single moms need better role models. In *The Price of Justice in America*, I suggested Barack Obama and Colin Powell could serve such roles, to which I would add sportsmen like Kareem Abdul-Jabbar, Michael Jordan and Shaquille O'Neal. These well-known personalities could also be supplemented by the personal touch of some Big Brothers who extricated themselves from the ghettos.

➢ Young black girls need better access to long-term contraceptives that would decrease the extremely high rate of teen pregnancies which trap single moms in the welfare system. For example, Oprah and Venus and Serena Williams might be great role models to inspire them to demand more of themselves, as might Condoleezza Rice or even Michelle Obama.

The Racial Divide: Desegregation and Affirmative Action[269]

Although tackling violent crime in high crime urban communities suggests that this problem is predominantly a black problem, discrimination against blacks by whites has continued to be a constant source of friction.

What is the source of that friction currently?

It is not bigotry, since slavery has been ended for well over a century, and so has the Civil War. Certainly some whites are bigots, but they are in the minority.

The main reason for the friction is likely due to the lingering effects of desegregation. Cultural and economic differences between different groups likely added to the natural tendency of different groups to self-segregate themselves. Desegregation flew in the face of that tendency and resulted in major friction, and the lingering effects of desegregation have persisted.

Desegregation was intended to provide a means toward a long-term greater integration of the races. It was based on the presumption that children of different races growing up together would not be subject to the same sort of racial intolerance as their parents.

Yet desegregation in the 50s, 60s and 70s caused a white backlash. Whites exhibited some of their most shameful feelings of hatred in response to the bussing of black students in places like Little Rock, Chicago, and Boston, among many other cities. In hindsight, this reaction could have been predicted. White parents particularly resented and resisted having their children bussed out of their neighborhoods with decent schools to faraway poor schools with large minorities. Even when desegregation was carried out, students from different races still tended to self-segregate, though at least they became more familiar with and perhaps less fearful of each other, rather than remaining clueless.

It is difficult to end segregation, as I'll discuss next.

The Difficulty of Ending Segregation

Segregation may be difficult to ever stop. Most U.S. cities are carved into ethnic neighborhoods, because people from different ethnic backgrounds prefer to preserve their culture and easy access to ethnic foodstuffs. Even blacks often prefer to remain among their own. It would take massive governmental intervention of the kind mandated in Singapore, where nearly everyone lives in nice public housing and is subject to governmental regulation, to produce the kind of positive change promised by desegregation. That certainly is unlikely to happen here because we value free choice too much.

Whites are too often ignorant of the plight of blacks and sometimes too smug in thinking themselves superior. Our reputation as a cultural melting pot is due to a great extent to our ability to embrace hard-working immigrants who want to improve their children's chances to lead a good life. By the same token, whites should consider hard working blacks who can afford to move into middle class white communities in the same light as hard-working immigrants, rather than just judging them by their skin color. For the same reason, whites should resist the temptation to abandon neighborhoods after a few blacks or immigrants move in. If they stayed, housing prices would be less likely to depreciate.

Learning from the Military

An idea to promote more integration might be to use as a model the military's success in molding racially desegregated teams that function well in their mission, particularly for young men more at risk of criminality. These teams are organized based on creating a team with the needed skills, since the military does not employ affirmative action. Accordingly, its experience provides a great testament to the benefits of racial integration, since this blending of different ethnic and racial groups shows how mixed groups not only can get along but can learn and grow from an introduction to each other's cultures and ideas.

To a great extent the military's emphasis on teamwork contributed to acceptance of minority groups in the unit. By the same token, it is likely that a greater emphasis on teamwork in job performance would similarly be beneficial for integrating the workforce.

Still another possibility for furthering integration might be providing more pre-job training for unskilled workers or for prisoners about to be released. And it, too, might be modeled after the military's approach which is based on desegregation in a boot camp-type training. Rather than employing affirmative action to gain preconceived results, each recruit is considered equally and is judged based on performance alone, with no special dispensation due to being in a particular racial or ethnic group. Moreover, it is likely that private sources would contribute to supporting such training efforts because individuals would be judged on merit and skills in order to prepare them for jobs in different industries.

The Nationality and Language Divide[270]

The existence of multiple languages and cultures in the U.S. is another source of tension, particularly between groups that are in close contact with one another. This also occurs where a recently arrived cultural or language group has been growing, causing the group already there to perceive an economic and social threat.

For example, our porous Southern border has resulted in a prolonged influx of illegal immigrants over the years such that it is now estimated that there are over 11 million illegal Hispanic immigrants in the U.S. Many were desperately seeking sanctuary from horrific violence in Mexico and Central America, and many more were simply seeking a better life for themselves and their families in the face of very high unemployment in their countries of origin. Many Hispanics also came to work here just to send money back to their families. Often they take jobs that Anglos would disdain – backbreaking farm labor at very low wages, while sleeping in horrific housing, or work in the restaurant and housekeeping industries, again at very low wages. More problematic are day laborers in the construction industry, because these workers more directly compete with Americans for these jobs and are willing to work for less pay.

As a consequence of this economic pressure and threatened job loss due to immigrant workers willing to work for less, resentment among white Americans has grown, along with anger for other reasons. One such gripe is that illegal immigrants take big bites out of our social services, for example, in healthcare and in education. They avoid medical care because they cannot afford it. Because of their lower income and cultural resistance to medical care, they often wait until they are seriously ill and arrive in Emergency Departments requiring very expensive treatments. Because they have more children than Anglos, their children are consuming an ever increasing share of the national education budget. Affirmative action has also included Hispanics, another source of Anglo resentment.

But probably the biggest gripe of all is that Hispanics speak a different language and often make little attempt to assimilate. Like most immigrants from other cultures, they are more comfortable among their own, as witnessed by the myriad of ethnic neighborhoods in our major cities. First generation immigrants experience some difficulties adjusting to the new culture in the U.S., but for the most part they manage. Their children, second generation immigrants, have an easier time since they are educated in U.S. schools and are often indistinguishable from U.S. citizens in terms of English ability and even accents.

However, Hispanics have been treated differently. Bilingual education has been permitted and even encouraged in certain communities. While this may expedite initial education of immigrant children, it results in a diversion of education funds away from the children of Anglo citizens. And bilingual education may actually have slowed the progress of these children in assimilating into our culture. This is a pity, since Hispanic family values conform far better to those of American conservatives than to those of American liberals.

Anglo resentment of Hispanics has made immigration reform much more difficult, despite the agreed-upon need for so-called comprehensive immigration reform. No one agrees what constitutes comprehensive, except that it has to include the 11 million who are undocumented. Anglos despise the notion that illegal immigrants may be granted amnesty. Many Anglos prefer that illegal immigrants be deported or self-deport.

The Wall

Another point of contention is the border between the U.S. and Mexico, which has been a route for illegal immigration that has included drug traffickers and other criminals. In turn, the proposed building of a wall between the two countries has created even more tension. This has increased since President Trump has continued to support his campaign promise to build a truly high wall along our entire Southern border. This in turn has provoked resentment among Hispanics, both in the U.S. and in Mexico.

The Wall conjures up images of the Great Wall of China, which may have successfully served to keep out foreign invaders, but now is just a tourist attraction.

In more recent times, walls have become both a physical barrier and an emotional issue. One only has to look at other walls elsewhere to see that.

The Berlin Wall dividing East and West Germany kept a defeated rogue nation divided for about 45 years and became a big emotional symbol dividing Capitalism and Communism, both for Germans and for the rest of the world. Unlike other walls, it was designed to keep its citizens in, not to keep outsiders out. It served its purpose but was hated. It has been laced with graffiti and become another tourist attraction.

An even more recent example is the Wall dividing Israel and the West Bank. That wall, when coupled with perceived Israeli land grabs and no progress toward an independent Palestinian state, has caused extreme resentment among Palestinians. That resentment has in turn caused consequent condemnation in most of the international community.

So walls can work, but they come at a cost, both financial and in terms of public relations. Furthermore, unless adequately manned or monitored, they can be traversed by those healthy enough with ladders, ropes, or tunnels. Those in charge of securing our border actually advocate structures that permit visibility through them for better monitoring, which would probably reduce cost. But then consider that Mexicans have become expert at building tunnels to go underneath the border. Even Israelis have difficulty locating all the tunnels Palestinians have built along their short border. It will be much harder to locate all the tunnels that might be built along our 1800 mile border with Mexico.

However, none of this takes into account that the flow of immigrants across the Southern border has diminished greatly in the last several years. The Mexican economy has flourished, leading so many immigrants to return that there is no net influx of Hispanics into the U.S. anymore, and likely even a small net flow back into Mexico. And since the President's inauguration, border patrols indicate that illegal border crossings have decreased a further 40%. Under these circumstances, is the Wall even necessary? Is it worth the 40 billion dollars estimated that it would take to construct? Will Mexico ever pay for the cost of it?

The Wall has also incensed Mexico and the vast majority of Hispanics, who make up 16% of the U.S. population. Bearing in mind that this represents about 50 million people, the majority of whom are legal immigrants, this is a high price to pay. The future price for Republicans may be even higher, when in a few decades whites become a minority in the U.S.

Alternatives to the Wall

There are alternatives to the Wall. Border patrol agents recommend some sort of fencing and better monitoring. The President has proposed additional border patrol agents, and that may make more sense than the Wall.

Another possibility is that all this discussion of the wall and deportation will simply ratchet up fear in the Hispanic community, fear of Immigration and Customs Enforcement (ICE) agents knocking on their doors in the middle of the night and fear of mass deportations. We will never be able to identify and deport all 11 million, but we may be capable of generating enough fear in the Hispanic community that many will self-deport and return to a Mexico that is now better off than when they left it. The political price for such a strategy will be high, but probably no higher than building the Wall.

Former President George W. Bush (43) has voiced concerns about the Trump immigration stance. On the whole, it might be better for everyone to revisit Bush-era proposals, even including possible difficult paths to citizenship, or devising some compromise comprehensive immigration reform. Or what about a pathway to legal, non-voting status rather than citizenship for current illegal immigrants, perhaps coupled to some fines and an end of affirmative action for Hispanics?

Geographical and Political Divides[271]

The numerous geographical and political divides in America are another source of tension. These include the divisions between the North and South, the Coast and Middle America, and rural and urban residents. In addition there are ethnic and generational divisions and divisions due to income inequality. Here's a brief overview of those different divisions.

The North-South Divide

Even 150 years after the Civil War, the South smarts. Whites in the South were humiliated. Their way of life was taken away from them. They had to endure free blacks. Northern carpetbaggers further ravaged the South economically.

But Southerners slowly got their revenge. After President Lyndon Baines Johnson, they virtually exiled Democrats from the South, yet more Southern Democrats became Presidents than Northern Democrats. The South has contributed mightily to the economic decline of the Rust Belt by recruiting companies with cheaper non-union labor. Southerners also form the Bible Belt and are considerably more conservative than most Northerners. While the South can reliably be counted on to vote Republican, the South doesn't make up enough of the country to elect a President by itself.

The Divide between the Coasts and Middle America

A second, more critical geographical distinction currently is that between the Midwest and the Coasts. It is reflected in the division between the red states, which largely vote conservative and Republican, and the blue states, which largely vote liberal and Democratic.

Generally speaking, the Midwest and South reliably vote Republican, while the only states that reliably vote Democratic are those on the West Coast and East Coast in the Northeast. About the only reliably Democratic states in the Midwest are Minnesota and Illinois.

The Rural-Urban Divide

A third geographical divide is between rural and urban America. On electoral maps, this divide shows up in many states as a sea of red Republican-voting regions dotted with a few small blue Democratic-voting islands.

This rural-urban divide is also played out in economic disparities between the two areas. Cities have traditionally represented the apex of our civilizations, as exemplified by Athens and Rome. This tradition has continued in Europe, which has maintained the vibrancy of its cities and made it difficult for immigrants to live there, but easier for them to live in impoverished suburbs.

In the U.S., the economic division between urban and rural areas is reversed, since many cities were abandoned by white flight to the suburbs. U.S. cities remain business hubs, but their downtown areas are often deserted at nights and on weekends. This has been changing in some city neighborhoods where gentrification has been occurring, such as in "progressive" Boston, Seattle, New York, and San Francisco, where a downtown nightlife has flourished.

However, this increased infusion of wealth into certain areas has led to a division within these cities, since gentrification also excludes the poor. As a result, at the same time that parts of the cities have become a magnet for wealthy and well-paid high tech employees, the impoverished inner city slums have been growing in other parts of the same cities due to the fallout from the growing divide between rich and poor in America. So gentrification may help reclaim downtown areas of some cities, but it does not result in significant desegregation. In fact, it can make things worse, much worse, such as in San Francisco, Oakland and some other metropolitan areas that are suffering from a crisis of insufficient housing, exploding housing costs, and a growing homeless problem marked by tent cities, drugs and crime.

Rural and urban America are completely different, and this may be the most fundamental cultural divide of all. Their values are vastly different. Rural America is more religious and more conservative. Rural Americans work longer hours, believe in self-sufficiency and disdain handouts.

Rural America is much closer to nature and to the land, including farmlands and pasture. Rural America feeds urban America.

By comparison, urban America provides most business, jobs, and shopping malls.

It costs much more to live in urban America, due to rapidly escalating real estate prices. Urban Americans get almost all of their food from the local supermarket or fast food franchises, whereas rural Americans can feed themselves less expensively by farming and hunting.

These divisions are much more than economic. They are based in deep social and cultural difference, too, since urban America tends to dismiss and disparage rural America for not keeping up with the times and having old-fashioned values. Conversely, rural America sees in urban America a world of chaos and corruption exemplified by the false values of Hollywood and materialism.

Given this rural-urban divide, it may be more important to permit separate urban and rural rights than to emphasize the power of states' rights. The crime problem is very different in rural and urban America, largely because of the concentration of crime in urban America in the inner city slums. And given these differences, what may reduce crime in rural areas is much less likely to work in urban areas. Separate court systems may be appropriate for rural and urban America.

Other Divides[272]

Ethnic Divides

Naturally, there are other divides as well. To some extent, different ethnicities colonized different parts of the country, often reflecting different cultures and values. This may explain why my wife of German extraction assimilated well in Texas, which had a lot of German immigrants in the 1800s, but has hardly been accepted in Arkansas, which has a lot of Scots-Irish.

There are also different cultural attitudes toward the right to bear arms guaranteed by the second amendment. These cultural attitudes likely arose from ethnic differences and may not only reflect different attitudes towards guns, but also to associated violence which may have contributed to the higher rates of assault deaths in the Deep South than in New England.[273]

Generational Divides

The generational divides have increasingly become a source of conflict, even politically, because of the emphasis on youth in America and the devaluation of the values of older generations. This divide is furthered by the rapid pace of technological development which has been embraced by the younger generation, while leaving many older Americans behind.

For example, folks in my generation who were raised by European parents experienced much stricter discipline in growing up and were required to be more respectful of their elders, whereas parents in later generations have become far more lenient toward their children.

Our society celebrates youth and often shows little respect for those who are older, other than those in high positions of authority.

Age discrimination affects a lot of people. For instance, businesses prefer to hire younger staff to whom they can pay lower salaries. Each subsequent generation has been pigeonholed and labeled: baby boomers, gen-Xers, millennials, and centennials. The particular labels don't matter, but the labeling process reflects the great divide between the generations that is especially marked in much of the U.S.

How to Understand the Generational Divide

Currently, only two groups appear to really understand the different motivations, aspirations, and fears that drive each of these generational categories.

One group consists of businessmen and advertisers who are marketing products and their advertisements to specific groups, because they need this understanding to position and market their products successfully.

The other group consists of pollsters who gather data for the benefit of politicians, since the politicians need to target their message to appeal to these different groups.

Thus, the only way the rest of us will recognize and come to understand our generational differences is if we call on advertisers and pollsters to educate us.

How to Overcome the Generational Divide

How did we develop this generational divide and what can we do about it?

One factor is the emphasis on individualism in the United States and the high level of mobility, which tends to break up the family. For example, U.S. businesses encourage and reward mobility on the part of their workers. Consequently, the U.S. family is by and large a nuclear one: only two generations in the household, parents and children.

By contrast, Hispanic, European and Asian families here and in their home countries are far more likely to have several generations living under the same roof or within close proximity to each other. That closeness leads to greater understanding, appreciation, respect and cooperation among the generations that is sorely lacking for U.S. families.

Family-owned businesses are also affected. For example, the era of the family farm is largely over. The absence of other work nearby has led to younger generations of farm families abandoning the land in favor of greater job opportunities in cities, rendering the family farm an endangered species. Putting further pressure on the family farm is economic pressure from large corporate farm operations which are able to generate greater efficiencies of scale than a small farm, thereby rendering the family farm a nearly extinct species.

Intergenerational living under the same roof doesn't happen very much here, despite a trend for millennials who have trouble finding jobs to return to the family roost temporarily. As a result, individuals of one generation tend to associate with others of the same generation and to become increasingly isolated and less understanding of the needs and wishes of other generations.

To overcome these divides, grown children of retired parents should be encouraged, perhaps with tax credits, to take in their parents if their parents are willing to live with them. Grandparents are a great resource to help in raising children. Retirees are often suffering financially for lack of sufficient retirement savings, but their children could step in and pay them back a measure for their upbringing by taking care of their parents in those parents' declining years. Conversely, parents in their empty nest years, generally in their late 30s, 40s, and 50s, might help their children who are struggling financially by taking them in while they get on their feet.

Much greater attention should also be given to the ways that Hispanic families benefit from several generations living under the same roof. Even if it is not feasible for most Anglos to accommodate their parents, they may learn some of the positive benefits of greater association with those of other generations. This could be accomplished by encouraging volunteer work dedicated specifically to helping those of other generations.

Income Inequality

Another major source of division is the growing income inequality in America. Just recently a charity soliciting donations pointed out that eight super wealthy individuals own as much wealth as the poorest half of the people in the world! That poorest half is composed of 3.6 billion members, while 6 of the 8 richest are Americans: Jeff Bezos, Bill Gates, Warren Buffett, Mark Zuckerberg, Larry Ellison and Michael Bloomberg. This is certainly a stark picture of the vast gulf between rich and poor caused by the great inequality divide.

Listening to the President, you'd think the U.S. has lost its greatness. Yet a Global Wealth Report 2015 by Allianz, a major financial services firm, lists the top 10 countries in terms of their percentages of total global wealth:

United States – 41.6%	France	-	3.5%
China	- 10.5%	Canada	-	3.0%
Japan	- 8.9%	Italy	-	2.9%
U.K.	- 5.6%	Australia	-	2.0%
Germany	- 3.9%	South Korea	-	1.9%

As you can see, the U.S. holds almost half the world's wealth. No other country even comes close, not even China. The sum of the top 4 countries in Western Europe (15.9%) doesn't even generate half of our wealth. No wonder 6 of the world's 8 richest people are Americans. This might be a list we Americans could be proud of.

But the U.S. is also at the top of the list in terms of income inequality. Over the past 50 years the rich are getting richer in the U.S. while the poor are getting poorer.

Why Is There So Much Inequality in America?

In part, this economic divide is due to our pride in our system of capitalism and our values of individualism and freedom. Our ideal is that individuals can make themselves who they want to be by having clear goals for success and hard work, and they can ignore the real barriers many face to getting ahead. These barriers include not having the funds to secure an education necessary to move up the economic ladder. Our ideal also downplays the real advantages that come from having a high income family which is well connected.

At the same time, we disparage others who are not successful by claiming they have certain flaws that prevent them from getting ahead and so deserve whatever bad experience comes their way. For example, we pride ourselves on the fruit of our labor and don't feel that those lazier than ourselves deserve as much.

Meanwhile, many accept the proposition that the wealthy can use their money to control job opportunities for the poor and believe that trickle-down economics will actually lead to more jobs for workers, rather than further enriching those who are already wealthy. On the other hand, those who are disadvantaged don't believe that they are fairly reaping economic rewards, so management and labor are frequently at odds with each other.

Witness the ongoing debate about raising the minimum wage. Business owners are largely opposed, while workers are pushing for a higher living wage, especially in cities that have become increasingly expensive for workers to live, such as rapidly gentrifying San Francisco.

We thrive on the capitalist system and don't want to become as socialist as Western Europe with its expensive social safety net. However, we tend to overlook those who lose out as a result of this system in which the rich keep getting richer and the poor poorer. At the same time the middle class is whittled away and many formerly middle class individuals and families become impoverished. So shouldn't we be asking when is enough money enough? When do government or wealthy individuals need to intervene in order to help redistribute some of the wealth from those on the top, so those on the bottom can better survive and work towards their own success?

There is no doubt that great entrepreneurs have improved our lives and capabilities, and they should be rewarded. Steve Jobs did not live an opulent lifestyle, and neither does Warren Buffett. Wouldn't a billion dollars be enough? In fact, many billionaires seem to have come to this conclusion and are seeking to give their money away to worthwhile causes. One prominent example is Bill Gates, recently identified as the second richest man in the world, who has stopped trying to make money and is trying to figure out how best to give it away through the Bill and Melinda Gates Foundation. That's a lot of work, so Warren Buffett, the world's third richest man, asked Gates to give his money away as well. Almost certainly some of Gates' donations have been less successful than others, but then that is the nature of creating a system to offer money to needy individuals or causes.

There has also been a move by Warren Buffett to have wealthy philanthropists pledge to give away at least 50% of their fortunes. That may be admirable, but did these wealthy Americans need to amass so much wealth that they didn't know what to do with it? Is there something about our system that is so imbalanced that too much money goes to those who are already very wealthy or that some corporate leaders make 300 times as much as their employees?

These fabulously successful entrepreneurs reach a point where they realize they need to do something philanthropic with the money they generated, to put the excess money they don't need to some good use. They have much less experience and proficiency in that area. As a result, they may make charitable investments that are not as beneficial as they could be. I say this despite the fact that I support Mark Zuckerberg and Priscilla Chen's pledge to commit $3 billion to cure disease. Their effort seems to be starting by rewarding high risk, high reward research that the National Institutes of Health (NIH) is unlikely to fund.

One question many ask is why super rich individuals feel a need to keep on making more and more money and never seem satisfied with enough. They may be good at it, but is that any reason to continue *ad infinitum*? Certainly they may need to reinvest in a successful business enterprise to keep it going, so I'm not suggesting that individuals and businesses shouldn't benefit from having healthy profit margins.

Rather, I'm talking about a psychological addiction to making money that may be akin to an addiction to gambling. Gambling addictions are destructive to the individual with the addiction. An addiction to making money[274] would fall in the same category, known as process addictions.[275] It may be less destructive to the individual but could be quite destructive to society.

Some Ways to Fix the Income Inequality Problem

Given this huge problem of income inequality, I suggest two possible remedies:

➢ Re-education, training centers and retreats.

➢ A cap to limit individuals from amassing wealth beyond a certain sum

Here's how and why I think these remedies would work.

First, re-education, training centers, and retreats should be established for those few individuals who are completely consumed with making money for its own sake. While these are designed to be treatment centers, they should be given another more socially acceptable name for those in power, so they don't have to think of themselves as having any kind of disturbance requiring psychological treatment.

Since these centers would only be designed for a relatively small group of people – the super-wealthy who are guided by making money to the exclusion of other motivators, we probably wouldn't need more than one or two high-quality retraining centers.

Funding for such a center should be very high, since its occupants are used to luxury, and probably the funding could come from the very rich, since they have the means to pay for the very best. As in other education, training, and treatment centers, like-minded individuals with a similar compulsion, could empathize with each other and help each other along the journey toward changing their way of life, much like groups like Gamblers Anonymous help individuals maintain their commitment to change and self-improvement.

Second, some sort of cap should be established to limit individuals from amassing wealth beyond a certain sum, whether that is $1 billion, $5 billion or $10 billion. Any additional income earned would have 92% of it turned over to the government for social programs or to a choice among specific charities from a government-approved list. Why 92%? Because that was the top tax rate during the Eisenhower administration for those earning over what would be about $3.5 million now.[276] Remember, that was when America was truly great---shortly after World War II.

The social programs to be considered should be ones for the poor that have been demonstrated to be effective in raising them out of poverty through their own work and initiative, thereby further reducing income inequality. What should the criteria be for what charities are eligible for such donations? These donations should either benefit everyone, or most benefit those in greatest need, again since this would decrease income inequality the most. If so desired, the government-approved list could require that all such charities put America first.

A Threatening Gender Divide

There has always been a gender gap in pay, and in the past year, this male-female divide has become even stronger, because of more sexual misconduct allegations. The first of these allegations, such as against Harvey Weinstein and Roger Ailes, resulted in an outcry against them, leading to their fall from power, and as more and more women came forward, this helped to spark the #MeToo movement that has been gathering steam and may affect the 2018 mid-term elections. Numerous politicians like Al Franken and John Conyers have fallen from grace as a result, and more and more women have been running for office. TV moguls and producers like Leslie Moonves and Bill Shine, and celebrities such as Charley Rose, Bill O'Reilly and Matt Lauer have fallen from grace as a result. Bill Cosby was even thrown in prison with a 3 to 10 year sentence.

This divide was most dramatically reflected in the Senate hearings for the confirmation of Justice Brett Kavanagh which riveted the country as a result of the allegations made against him by Christine Blasey Ford. These and other allegations upended the confirmation process, cast doubt on the ability of the Supreme Court to avoid partisanship, and further widened the divide between men and women.

This growing divide could potentially endanger family stability by turning husbands and wives against each other as this drama plays out over the next years in America. Only time will tell how serious the likelihood of this divide is to undermine male-female relationships and the stability of American society.

Why We Still Need Each Other[277]

Whether they realize it or not, to one extent or other those on each side of these divides need each other. The need is not always mutual. Without a doubt, the poor need the rich more than the rich need the poor. The older generation certainly needs and should get help from the younger generations. Although the younger generations often manage on their own better than their parents do, some do need an occasional assist from mom and dad. By the same token, parents of younger children could benefit from having live-in or nearby grandparents to help raise children.

Different ethnic regions of the country and the North/South divide still have some need of each other. The South benefits from the North because federal taxes subsidize the South more than it pays in, and even with that help, the South is much poorer. The North still needs the South for some of its agricultural products. The Coasts need the Midwest for their farms and livestock, and the Midwest needs the Coasts in order to ship their products internationally and to import the products it needs. Heaven help the U.S. if California, the fifth largest economy in the world,[278] or the whole West Coast, decided to secede.

The greatest co-dependence is exhibited by rural and urban America. Rural America would not survive without hungry urban America there to buy its goods. Urban America could only survive without rural America if it imported all its food, which would seriously raise urban food prices.

Yet these two Americas do not appreciate each other, and that leads to the disaffection exhibited by our two party political system. Instead, urbanites need to appreciate the hard work and work ethic of rural Americans. Rural Americans need to acknowledge their dependence on Urban America for consumption of their bounty, for commerce in general and for tax supports.

The Increasing Incivility and Toxicity of the System

This two party system recently has become increasingly uncivil and toxic. That toxicity has led to tribalism, whereby politicians in each party show allegiance to their tribe more than to their constituents or country. Cooperation is nearly nonexistent, collaboration nearly extinct. Collaborators, a dirty word in World War II, have been eclipsed by competitors, a trademark of our capitalist society. Thus, bipartisanship seems to be dead or dying, splitting us further apart, with the risk of a new Civil War, which some journalists even write about.[279]

Another reason for this incivility and toxicity is that money has become paramount, and no amount seems to be enough, even for the richest among us. That greed has created increasing economic inequality and much suffering, anguish and anger. Compromise could be a solution,[280] but tribalism fights even that. The country is divided, yet each side in turn claims a "mandate" with every presidential election, even if they lose the popular vote. Most recently this has been reflected in the loss of Democrats like Al Gore and Hillary Clinton, due to the Electoral College system, despite winning the popular vote. In effect, it gave rural Republican voters an edge over predominantly urban Democratic voters.

The Electoral College, whatever its merits, has unfortunately deprived most Americans of the value of their vote, whether they live in Red States or Blue States. In both cases, their votes are taken for granted. Only votes of citizens of so-called battleground states are seriously courted or contested, because only their votes can sway an election. In the 2016 election, the 10 consensus battleground states had a combined total of 132 electoral college votes out of a total of 538 (only 24.5%). The remaining 75% of voters were effectively disenfranchised; their issues didn't count as much. The Electoral College should be reformed so as to make Presidential candidates appeal to voters in all states.

The absence of a willingness to compromise is the single biggest roadblock to making America great again. It's also the single biggest impediment to criminal justice reform. And ultimately it could lead to the collapse of the political system in Washington, which probably cannot long endure favorability ratings under 20%. The election of President Trump demonstrated voter disaffection with both political parties. While over a million disaffected women came to Washington to protest the Trump presidency, it is likely that a million Trump supporters might have descended on Washington with their own march of disapproval had Hillary Clinton won.

Some Ways to Reform the System

Is there anything that can turn that divisiveness and inter-group hostility around? There is, but it will take extensive work beginning with seeking mutual understanding and compromise. Each side has to attempt to understand what most matters to and motivates the other side, whether older vs. younger, rich vs. poor, white vs. black, southern vs. northern, rural vs. urban, conservative vs. liberal, or Republican vs. Democrat. If we don't seek this understanding and compromise, the country will continue to swing back and forth between extremist positions on the two sides, and the hostilities might even escalate further, resulting in severe economic and social damage to our country.

What is really needed is a more objective look into the issues that divide the two sides to help decide how to break the impasses. In *The Price of Justice in America*, I started to consider these possible solutions. In that book, I used correlation analysis to come to the conclusion that liberals were mistaken about gun ownership being the primary cause of violent crime and homicides. I found instead that poor blacks in urban ghettos contributed the most to violent crime, and that blacks needed to concentrate more on how to reduce black-on-black killings, which considerably outnumber police killings of blacks, the focus of the Black Lives Matter movement.

If the current need to raise funds for reelection efforts could be reduced, that would help, since both sides are at fault in spending too much money on these races. Yet neither side in power is willing to change the status quo. They each seem to try to raise more and more money, believing that the campaign with the most money is more likely to win, and campaign debt can be paid off after the election. But a huge spending spree at election time doesn't always work. Witness the loss of Hillary Clinton, who lost despite spending much more than Donald Trump. And several millionaire businessmen like Mike Huffington and Meg Whitman spent millions on their failed bids for office in California.

As a result of these financial excesses, campaign finance reform is very badly needed to reduce the corroding influence of money from big money donors seeking favorable treatment and the wastefulness of huge sums spent on elections by both parties.

Aside from these considerations, campaign finance reform to reduce expenses would cut down on the time legislators spend at phone banks soliciting contributions. Instead, they would have considerably more time to attend to the people's business.[281] One can only hope for campaign finance reform, now that the President has shown that a candidate can win while being outspent by far more money raised by Hillary Clinton.

Changes in procedural rules might also be implemented to encourage bipartisan action and compromise, as suggested by political insiders like former Oklahoma GOP Congressman Mickey Edwards.[282] Unfortunately, such changes can only be made by D.C. politicians, who don't seem to be inclined to make any changes to rein in political influence.

Still, there is an outcry for change that was manifested in the 2016 election, and it should be heeded by both parties in order to gain popular support for what Congress and the President are doing. Otherwise, the next years will only be filled with more upheavals, especially in light of divisive concerns that the Presidential election may have been undermined and possibly delegitimized by Russian hacking, not to mention liberal outcries regarding Republican insistence on voter I.D. requirements and the repeal of Obamacare.

The outcry for change was not only exhibited by Trump supporters, but also by Bernie Sanders supporters before he lost the Democratic primary to Hillary Clinton. The public is angry about gridlock in Washington and the failure of federal politicians to serve Main Street instead of Wall Street. They don't agree with the huge salaries and bonuses for CEOs, when their own standard of living is stagnant or receding. They have shown that they are desperate enough to elect a very wealthy non-politician as President. There is also concern that the President's appointment of other billionaires to cabinet level positions may signal less willingness to help the little guy on Main Street than Candidate Trump's campaign promises.

Both political parties are in disarray as a result of the public anger and the election. Traditional Democrats, who came out on the short end of the stick when Hillary Clinton lost, will face a serious challenge from former Bernie Sanders supporters, perhaps with support from Elizabeth Warren.

There is also some pressure on the Republicans to change, in spite of their unexpected sweep of all three branches of government. Triumphant Republicans should not simply assume that the election of President Trump validates their position. Only a few weeks before the election, their party was very divided and could become so again if the Mueller probe derails the President. If not, the President and many Republicans have still been beset by continuing scandals about corruption and bad behavior. This is reflected in the continued charges of malfeasance initiated by Democrats and the ongoing investigations of Russian hacking by Robert Mueller and others encouraged by the Democrats. Most notably, the divisions were starkly shared on the nationally and internationally televised rancorous Senate hearings on the confirmation of Brett Kavanaugh to the Supreme Court. While he was ultimately confirmed, his appointment has resulted in a likely backlash of women voters and media second guessing of the judgments he makes along with the rest of the Supreme Court.

Conservatives also face being drowned by a Tsunami when whites become a minority in the country in a few decades. If the current Congress and Administration don't reach out sincerely and successfully to blacks, Hispanics, and women, no amount of voter registration requirements or mass deportations will prevent the flood of anger that is likely to be unleashed at the voting booth in the future.

All told, there are a lot of reasons for Americans of different political stripes to work together to achieve a more united country to contribute to the success of all. The President may be able to govern the country despite this divisiveness, but his successors may not.

Even the news media can play a role. They are not all fake, though most have a liberal bias. Whether their bias is liberal or conservative, it is reflected in the opinions expressed by their news anchors and by the guests brought on to comment on news and talk shows. While the media sometimes pretend to show both sides of an issue by inviting spokespersons for the other side to participate in discussions or debates, the host or moderator always makes it clear what side the TV station and its viewers are on.

However, the news media could contribute to bipartisanship and reduce the divisions by inviting speakers who have a more neutral position and who offer commonsense proposals on an issue from a compromise or more bipartisan perspective. Talk radio should do the same.

It may take a talk or news show producer more work to identify such individuals, but they should do it, because bipartisanship can work. A glowing example of this is the recent nearly unanimous (98-1) passage of a Senate bill to address the opioid crisis.[283] Among other things, the bill will create a grant program for comprehensive recovery centers for drug treatment, permit Medicaid coverage for such treatment, and require the U.S. Postal Service to screen packages for fentanyl if they have been shipped from overseas.

Another possible way to generate more bipartisanship suggested itself during the contentious Senate hearings to confirm

214

Justice Kavanaugh. A simple majority is now required for confirmation of justices, not a supermajority as before. If a supermajority (60% or 67%) of House or Senate members were required for passage of bills, that requirement would force their members to pass more bipartisan legislation or risk losing re-election because they didn't manage to get anything done. Indeed, at least 14 state legislatures already have such supermajority requirements to pass bills that increase taxes.[284]

If the current divisiveness is not ameliorated, the grim alternative is to face the prospect of deterioration and decline which no one wants. We shouldn't want to wait for the next race riot to heed these words of a less-than-saintly Rodney King appealing for calm during a 1992 race riot: "People, I just want to say, you know, can we all get along?"

POSTSCRIPT

At last! Since the writing of this book, criminal justice reform legislation in The First Step act was passed by the U.S. Senate by a vote of 87 to 12 on December 18, 2018, by the House on December 20 by a vote of 358 to 36, and signed into law by President Trump on December 21. Even with all sorts of other politically divisive issues swirling in Washington, our elected officials can still work together in a bipartisan fashion if the issue is important enough for a consensus to be reached.

ABOUT THE AUTHOR

Paul Brakke is a scientist based in the Little Rock, Arkansas area. He became interested in studying the criminal justice system because his life was turned upside down by the system. This occurred after his wife was falsely accused of aggravated assault for allegedly trying to run some kids over with her car, since a group of kids and some neighbors wanted her out of the neighborhood. Eventually, the Brakkes were forced to move as part of a plea agreement, since otherwise, Brakke's wife was threatened with a possible 16 year jail sentence if the case went to trial and she lost.

He has previously told his wife's story along with a critique of the criminal justice system in his first book, *American Justice?*. After that, Brakke went on to look at other problems in the system and the country in general and how to fix them.

His other books include: *The Costly U.S. Prison System, Fixing the U.S. Criminal Justice System, Dealing with Illegal Immigrants and the Opioid Crisis, The Price of Justice, Cops Aren't Such Bad Guys*, and *The Great National Divides*. To publish them, he set up a publishing company, American Leadership Books, featuring books on criminal justice and social issues which are available in print and ebook format through Amazon, Ingram, Kindle, and other major distributors. Over the past five years, he has become an expert on the criminal justice system and a speaker and consultant on the topic.

Since these first books were directed primarily at law enforcement professionals, politicians and academics, Brakke is now developing a series of books on criminal justice to appeal to the general public, especially conservatives, beginning with *Crime in America*. The next books in the series will be shorter and will deal individually with prisons in America, the police, courts, illegal immigration, the opioid crisis, and racial divisions and conflicts.

The books' website is www.americanleadershipbooks.com. Audiobooks are available at https://audible.com/author/Paul-Brakke/B0714KG374.

FOR MORE INFORMATION AND FREE GIFTS,
INCLUDING PREVIEWS, CHAPTERS FROM NEW BOOKS, AND DISCOUNT COUPONS

http://www.americanleadershipbookspublishing.com

CONTACT US

For more information:

American Leadership Books
Little Rock, Arkansas
www.americanleadershipbooks.com
brakkep@gmail.com

NOTES

Chapter 1

[1] Excerpt from Chapter 1 of Brakke, *Dealing with Crime by Illegal Immigrants and the Opioid Crisis*.

[2] Stephen Dinan, "Illegals Commit Crimes at Double the Rate of Native-Born: Study," *Washington Times*, January 26, 2018.
https://www.washingtontimes.com/news/2018/jan/26/illegals-commit-crimes-double-rate-native-born-stu/

[3] Excerpt from Chapter 3 of Brakke, *Dealing with Crime by Illegal Immigrants and the Opioid Crisis*.

[4] See also Paul Brakke, *The Costly U.S. Prison System*, Preface, American Leadership Books, 2017.

[5] Excerpt from Chapter 4 of Brakke, *Dealing with Crime by Illegal Immigrants and the Opioid Crisis*.

[6] Rachel E. Morgan, "Race and Hispanic Origin of Victims and Offenders, 2012-15", U.S. Department of Justice, Bureau of Justice Statistics, Special Report, NCJ 250747.

[7] There are no values given in this row because the values within each column above cannot be added properly since they were normalized differently.

[8] Paul Brakke, *The Costly U.S. Prison System*, American Leadership Books, 2017.

[9] While it is not appropriate to compare results within a column or between columns from this table because different rows have been normalized differently, other data show that there are more white victims of each class of offender than victims of any other race/ethnicity.

[10] Excerpt from Chapter 6 of Brakke, *Dealing with Crime by Illegal Immigrants and the Opioid Crisis*.

[11] Excerpt from Chapter 6 of Brakke, *The Price of Justice in America*.

[12] Excerpt from Chapter 7 of Brakke, *The Price of Justice in America*.

[13] Excerpt from Chapter 8 of Brakke, *The Price of Justice in America*.

Chapter 2

[14] Alexa Lardieri, "Dramatic drop in Police Officer Deaths in 2017", *U.S. News & World Report*, https://www.usnews.com/news/national-news/articles/2017-12-28/dramatic-drop-in-police-officer-deaths-in-2017

[1515] Duren Banks, Joshua Hendrix, Matthew Hickman and Tracey Kyckelhahn, "National Sources of Law Enforcement Data", U.S. Department of Justice, Bureau of Justice Statistics, revised October 2016;
https://www.bjs.gov/content/pub/pdf/nsleed.pdf

[16] Josh Saul, "Police killed more than 1,100 people this year and a quarter of them were black", *Newsweek*, http://www.newsweek.com/police-shootings-killing-us-unarmed-black-reform-michael-brown-7644787

[17] United States Census Bureau, Quick Facts; https://www.census.gov/quickfacts/fact/table/US/PST045216

[18] Matthew Cella and Alan Neuhauser, "Race and Homicide in America, by the Numbers", *U.S. News & World Report*, September 29, 2016; https://www.usnews.com/news/articles/2016-09-29/race-and-homicide-in-america-by-the-numbers

[19] Ibid.

[20] Wesley Lowery, "Analysis: More whites killed by police but blacks 2.5 times more likely to be killed", *The Washington Post*, http://www.chicagotribune.com/news/nationworld/ct-police-shootings-race-20160711-story.html

[21] Ref. 18.

[22] In *Cops Aren't Such Bad Guys*, I discuss at length the difficulties police face during and after involvement in a killing of a suspect.

[23] Excerpt from Chapter 2 of Brakke, *The Price of Justice in America.*

[24] Excerpt from Chapter 1 of Brakke, *The Price of Justice in America.*

[25] Excerpt from Chapter 1 of Brakke, *Cops Aren't Such Bad Guys.*

[26] Lance LoRusso, *When Cops Kill,* Blue Line Lawyer, 2013.

[27] Lance LoRusso, *Blue News*, Blue Line Lawyer, 2016.

[28] John Swayne and Ciara McCarthy, "Killings by US Police Logged at Twice the Previous Rate Under New Federal Program."

[29] Excerpt from Chapter 2 of Brakke, *Cops Aren't Such Bad Guys.*

[30] Excerpt from Chapter 3 of Brakke, *Cops Aren't Such Bad Guys.*

[31] LoRusso, *When Cops Kill,* p. 32.

[32] LoRusso, *When Cops Kill,* p. 35.

[33] Ibid., p. 39.

[34] Ibid., pp. 40-41.

[35] Bob McManus, "Blame Only the Man Who Decided Tragically to Resist," *New York Post,* December 4, 2016. http://nypost.com/2014/12/04/eric-garner-was-a-victim-of-himself-for-deciding-to-resist

[36] Excerpt from Chapter 4 of Brakke, *Cops Aren't Such Bad Guys.*

[37] Peter Holley and Katie Zezima, "White Tulsa Officer Charged in Death of Unarmed Black Man, Freed on Bond, *The Washington Post,* September 23, 2016, https://www.washingtonpost.com/news/post-nation/wp/2016/09/22/tulsa-officer-who-fatally-shot-terrence-crutcher-charged-with-first-degree-manslaughter/?utm_term=.23e8d55b2bb1

[38] LoRusso, *Blue News,* pp. 5-9.

[39]Richard Johnson, "Examining the Prevalence of Deaths from the Police Use of Force," Criminal Justice Program, University of Toledo, December 26, 2014. http://www.slideshare.net/robertsearfoss33/police-lethal-forcepresentation

[40]Ibid.

[41] Excerpt from Chapter 3 of Brakke, *Fixing the U.S. Criminal Justice System.*

[42]http://apps.washingtonpost.com/g/documents/national/department-of-justice-report-on-the-ferguson-mo-police-department/1435

[43]Independent Lens, 4/8/13

[44] Brian M. Rosenthal, *Police Criticize Trump for Urging Officers Not to Be 'Too Nice' in Handling Suspects*, New York Times, 7/30/2017.

[45] Four additional solutions are suggested in this chapter of *Fixing the U.S. Criminal Justice System.*

[46] Excerpt from Chapter 7 of Brakke, *Fixing the U.S. Criminal Justice System.*

[47] Frank Fellone, "For Night Stops, Light Up Interior,"*Arkansas Democrat-Gazette*, September 16, 2017.

Chapter 3

[48] Excerpt from Chapter 1 of Brakke, *Fixing the U.S. Criminal Justice System.*

[49]Steven Nolan, "The Prison Industrial Complex", *The Intelhub.com*; http://theintelhub.com/2012/05/17prison-industrial-complex

[50]Robert A. Ferguson, *Inferno: An Anatomy of American Punishment*, Harvard University Press, 2014.

[51] Michelle Alexander, *The New Jim Crow: Mass Incarceration in the Age of Colorblindness*, The New Press, 2012.

[52] Charlie Rose; http://www.tv.com/shows/charlie-rose/watch/marion-cotillard-andrew-solomon-a-discussion-about-prison-reform-2615132

[53] David Wolman, "The New Economics of Crime and Punishment", http://www.wired.com/2012/11/st_essay_convictonomics

[54] Ed Morrisey, "Sessions: Food Stamps Programs Expanding in Costs, Size," *Hot Air*; http://hotair.com/archives/2012/06/27/sessions-food-stamp-programs-exploding-in-costs-size

[55] "1 in 3 Black Men Go To Prison? The 10 Most Disturbing Facts about Racial Inequality in the U.S. Criminal Justice System." *AlterNet*, March 17, 2012.

[56] "Families with Incarcerated Parents Fact Sheet."

[57] "The Caging of America: Why Do We Lock So Many People Up," *The New Yorker*, January 30, 2012; http://www.newyorker.com/arts/critics/atlarge/2012/01/30/120130crat_atlarge_gopnik

[58] https://static.prisonpolicy.org/scans/vera/the-price-of-prisons.pdf

[59] Office of Policy Planning and Research, United States Department of Labor, "The Negro Family: The Case for National Action", March 1965; http://www.intellectualtakeout.org/content/quotes-welfare-state-family

[60] Erik Eckholm, "With Higher Numbers of Prisoners Comes a Tide of Troubled Children," *New York Times,* July 5, 2009.

[61] Some financial estimates run over a trillion dollars (Carrie Pettus-Davis, Washington Univ. St. Louis, referred to by Matt Ferner,*The Full Cost Of Incarceration In The U.S. Is Over $1 Trillion, Study Finds* ;http://www.huffingtonpost.com/entry/mass-incarceration-cost_us_57d82d99e4b09d7a687fde21), and that's only the financial part.

[62] Excerpt from Chapter 4 of Brakke, *Fixing the U.S. Criminal Justice System.*

[63] John F. Pfaff, *Locked In, The True Causes of Mass Incarceration and How to Achieve Real Reform,* Basic Books, 2017.

[64] Kathleen Ridolfi and Maurice Possley "Preventable Error: A Report on Prosecutorial Misconduct in California 1997-2009" http://digitalcommons.law.scu.edu/ncippubs/2

[65] *Chicago Tribune,* http://www.chicagotribune.com/news/watchdog/chi-020103trial1,0,479347.story

[66]http://www.innocenceproject.org/news-events-exonerations/errant-prosecutors-seldom-held-to-account

[67] An additional solution is presented in this chapter of *Fixing the U.S. Criminal Justice System.*

[68] Mark Donald: Texas Lawyer, A Justice-at-All-Costs Attitude--Impact Player of the Year Craig Watkins, 12-24-2007; www.truthinjustice.org/craig-watkins.htm

[69] Excerpt from Chapter 6 of Brakke, *Fixing the U.S. Criminal Justice System.*

[70] Two additional suggested solutions are presented in this chapter of *Fixing the U.S. Criminal Justice System.*

Chapter 4:

[71] Excerpt from Chapter 1 of Brakke, *The Costly U.S. Prison System.*

[72] Graph: Courtesy of Prison Policy Initiative, 2017

[73] Ibid, Chapter 7.

[74] Elizabeth Hinton, *From the War on Poverty to the War on Crime: The Making of Mass Incarceration in America,* Harvard University Press, 2016, Chapters 2-3.

[75] Ibid, Chapters 4-9.

[76] James Kilgore, *Understanding Mass Incarceration: A People's Guide to the Key Civil Rights Struggle of Our Time,* The New Press, 2015, p. 18.

[77] Elizabeth Hinton, *From the War on Poverty to the War on Crime: The Making of Mass Incarceration in America,* Harvard University Press, 2016, Epilogue.

[78] Peter K. Enns, *Incarceration Nation: How the United States Became the Most Punitive Democracy in the World,* Cambridge University Press, 2016.

[79] Barry Latzer, *The Rise and Fall of Violent Crime in America,* Encounter Books, 2015.

[80] Peak criminal activity occurs around age 20.

[81] "Uniform Crime Reporting Statistics, estimated violent crime rate", U.S. Department of Justice, https://www.ucrdatatool.gov/Search/Crime/State/RunCrimeTrendsinOneVar.cfm ; U.S. Department of Justice, Bureau of Justice Statistics Bulletin "Prisoners 1925-81", https://www.bjs.gov/content/pub/pdf/p2581.pdf; "Prisoners in Custody of State or Federal Correctional Authorities 1977-98", http://www.bjs.gov/index.cfm?ty=pbdetail&lid=2080 ; "Prisoners in 2000", http://www.bjs.gov/index.cfm?ty=pbdetail&lid=927; "Prisoners in 2005", http://www.bjs.gov/index.cfm?ty=pbdetail&lid=912; "Prisoners in 2015", http://www.bjs.gov/index.cfm?ty=pbdetail&lid=5869

[82] This is one of the single strongest correlations that I have plotted among hundreds of such tests. It was totally unexpected and literally bowled me over when I encountered it.

[83] John F. Pfaff, *Locked In, The True Causes of Mass Incarceration and How to Achieve Real Reform,* Basic Books, 2017, pp. 129-130.

[84] Excerpt from Chapter 2 of Brakke, *The Costly U.S. Prison System.*

[85] Pfaff, *Locked In*, 2017, pp. 12, 97.

[86] Peter Wagner and Bernadette Rabuy, "Mass Incarceration: The Whole Pie 2017", Prison Policy Initiative, https://www.prisonpolicy.org/reports/pie2017.html

[87] Jen Fifield, "Many States Face Dire Shortage of Prison Guards", Pew Charitable Trusts/Research & Analysis/Stateline, 3/1/2016.

[88] However, the sum saved should be less than what an ex-con could save from working the same number of hours on a minimum wage job after being released. This is because the ex-con should always be incentivized to leave prison and work on the outside rather than succumbing to any temptation to remain in prison.

[89] "Last Days of Solitary", *PBS, Frontline,* April 18, 2017

[90] Kerik, *From Jailer to Jailed*, pp. 258-9.

[91] Shane Bauer, *American Prison. A Reporter's Undercover Journey into the Business of Punishment*, Penguin Press, 2018.

[92] Peter K. Enns, *Incarceration Nation: How the United States Became the Most Punitive Democracy in the World*, Cambridge University Press, 2016, chapter 7.

[93] Peter Wagner and Bernadette Rabuy, "Mass Incarceration: The Whole Pie 2017", Prison Policy Initiative, https://www.prisonpolicy.org/reports/pie2017.html

[94] It is very difficult to get national statistics regarding caseloads and turnover, so I have had to resort to using results from individual states.

[95] Cathy Frye, "Parole officers feeling the heat. Heavy caseloads ramp up stress; job turnover high", *Northwest Arkansas Democrat-Gazette*, 8/25/13.

[96] "Probation and Parole: A Primer for Law Enforcement Officers", Bureau of Justice Assistance, U.S. Department of Justice, 2009.

[97] Len Sipes, Kirsten Lewis and Adam Matz, "Stress and Turnover in Parole and Probation-APPA"; http://media.csosa.gov/podcast/audio/2014/03/stress-turnover-parole-and-probation-appa/

[98] Peter Wagner and Bernadette Rabuy, "Mass Incarceration: The Whole Pie 2017", Prison Policy Initiative, https://www.prisonpolicy.org/reports/pie2017.html

[99] Len Sipes, Kirsten Lewis and Adam Matz, "Stress and Turnover in Parole and Probation-APPA"; http://media.csosa.gov/podcast/audio/2014/03/stress-turnover-parole-and-probation-appa/

[100] Cathy Frye, "Parole officers feeling the heat. Heavy caseloads ramp up stress; job turnover high", *Northwest Arkansas Democrat-Gazette,* 8/25/13.

[101] Peter Wagner and Bernadette Rabuy, "Mass Incarceration: The Whole Pie 2017", Prison Policy Initiative, https://www.prisonpolicy.org/reports/pie2017.html

[102] "Probation and Parole: A Primer for Law Enforcement Officers", Bureau of Justice Assistance, U.S. Department of Justice, 2009.

[103] "Program Profile: Reduced Probation Caseload in Evidence-Based Setting (Iowa)", National Institute of Justice, July 17, 2012, https://www.crimesolutions.gov/ProgramDetails.aspx?ID=259

[104] "A History of Mental Institutions in the United States", *TikiToki*; http://www.tiki-toki.com/timeline/entry/37146/A-History-of-Mental-Institutions-in-the-United-States/#vars!date=1874-02-17_16:12:32!

[105] "Sweden Has Done for Its Prisoners What the U.S. Won't," https://mic.com/articles/109138/sweden-has-done-for-its-prisoners-what-the-u-s-won-t#.rKzDsN58s

[106] PBS News Hour, 12/13/2016.

[107] Sarah Varney, "By the numbers: Mental illness behind bars", *PBS News Hour* 5/15/2014.

[108] Bernard B. Kerik, *From Jailer to Jailed*, p. 280.

[109] Benjamin Hardy, "Dyslexia dysfunction", *Arkansas Times*, 6/9/2016.

[110] National Center for Learning Disabilities, "The State of Learning Disabilities", 2014.

[111] Jennifer Bronson, Laura M. Maruschak and Marcus Berzofsky, "Disabilities Among Prison and Jail Inmates," U.S. Department of Justice, Special Report, December 2015.

[112] Four additional observations and three recommendations are presented in this chapter of *The Costly U.S. Prison System.*

[113] Excerpt from Chapter 5 of Brakke, *The Price of Justice in America.*

[114] Excerpt from Introduction in Brakke, *The Costly U.S. Prison System.*

[115] Roy Walmsley, "World Prison Population List", 11th edition, World Prison Brief, Institute for Criminal Policy Research, Birkbeck University of London, 2016, http://www.prisonstudies.org/sites/default/files/resources/downloads/world_pris on_population_list_11th_edition_0.pdf

[116] NationMaster, "Crime>Violent Crime>Murder Rate per Million People: Countries Compared"; http://www.nationmaster.com/country-info/stats/Crime/Violent-crime/Murder-rate-per-million-people

[117] Violent crime is defined as homicide, rape, assault and robbery.

[118] John F. Pfaff, *Locked In, The True Causes of Mass Incarceration and How to Achieve Real Reform*, Basic Books, 2017, p. 177

[119] Data source: Department of Justice: http://www.ojp.doj.gov/bjs/correct.htm; International Centre for Prison Studies: http://www.kcl.ac.uk

Chapter 5

[120] Excerpt from Preface to Brakke, *The Costly U.S. Prison System.*

[121] Michael McLaughlin, Carrie Pettus-Davis, Derek Brown, Chris Veeh and Tanya Renn, "The Economic Burden of Incarceration in the U.S.", Working Paper #CI072016, Concordance Institute for Advancing Social Justice, George Warren Brown School of Social Work, Washington University in St. Louis, July, 2016.

[122] Bernard B. Kerik, *From Jailer to Jailed: My Journey from Correction and Police Commissioner to Inmate #84888-054*, Threshold Editions, 2015, p.126.

[123] Excerpt from Chapter 3 of Brakke, *The Costly U.S. Prison System.*

[124] NationMaster "Crime > Violent crime > Murder rate per million people: Countries Compared" http://www.nationmaster.com/country-info/stats/Crime/Violent-crime/Murder-rate-per-million-people

[125] Photo courtesy Alex Masi.

[126] Charles R. Larson,"Prisoner rehabilitation around the World", *Counterpunch*; http://www.counterepunch.org/2016/02/26/prisoner-rehabilitation-around-the-world

[127] Doran Larson, "Why Scandinavian Prisons are Superior", *The Atlantic,* 9/24/2013; http://www.theatlantic.com/international/archive/2013/09/why-scandinavian-prisons-are-superior/279949

[128] Rakesh Sharma, "3 Reasons This 'Perfect' Prison System Will Not Work in America", *The CheatSheet*, 5/22/2015; http://www.cheatsheet.com/business/3-reasons-why-norways-prison-system-should-not-be-replicated-in-america.html/?a=viewall

[129] Nicholas Turner and Jeremy Travis, "What We Learned from German Prisons", *New York Times*, 8/6/2015.

[130] Ram Subramanian and Alison Shames, "Sentencing and Prison Practices in Germany and the Netherlands: Implications for the United States", Vera Institute of Justice, 10/2013.

[131] Turner and Travis, "What We Learned from German Prisons"

[132] Subramanian and Shames, "Sentencing and Prison Practices in Germany and the Netherlands: Implications for the United States".

[133] Ibid.

[134] Subramanian and Shames, "Sentencing and Prison Practices in Germany and the Netherlands: Implications for the United States".

[135] Roy Walmsley, "World Prison Population List", 11th edition, World Prison Brief, Institute for Criminal Policy Research, Birkbeck University of London, 2016, http://www.prisonstudies.org/sites/default/files/resources/downloads/world_pris on_population_list_11th_edition_0.pdf

[136] Maire Gannon, "Crime Comparisons between Canada and the United States," Statistics Canada – Catalogue no. 85-002-XIE, vol. 21, no. 11.

[137] The Growth of Incarceration in the United States: Exploring Causes and Consequences, National Academies Press, Chapter 1.

[138] In 1995, violent crime rates in large urban areas were 907 per 100,000 compared to 1046 per 100,000 in rural areas. Tim Leonard, "Crime in Major Metropolitan Areas, 1991-1995," Statistics Canada – Catalogue no. 85-002-XPE, vol. 17, no. 5.

[139] Jocelyn Francisco and Christian Chenier, 'A Comparison Of Large Urban, Small Urban And Rural Crime Rates, 2005", Statistics Canada – Catalogue No. 85-002-XIE, vol. 27, no. 3.

[140] "Crime in the United States 2011," U.S. Department of Justice, Federal Bureau of Investigation, Criminal Justice Information Services Division, Table 16, https://ucr.fbi.gov/crime-in-the-u.s/2011/crime-in-the-u.s.-2011/tables/table_16_rate_number_of_crimes_per_100000_inhabitants_by_pop ulation_group_2011.xls

[141] "Demographics of Canada", Wikipedia; https://en.wikipedia.org/wiki/Demographics_of_Canada

[142] Mikhail Thomas, "Adult Criminal Court Statistics, 2003/04", Statistics Canada – Catalogue no. 85-002-XPE, vol. 24, no. 12.

[143] "Sourcebook of Criminal Justice Statistics," University at Albany, School of Criminal Justice, Hindelang Criminal Justice Research Center, http://www.albany.edu/sourcebook/tost_5.html#5_p

[144] Rebecca Johnstone and Jennifer Thomas, "Legal Aid in Canada: 1996-97", Statistics Canada – Catalogue no. 85-002-XIE, vol. 18, no. 10.

[145] Donald J. Farole, Jr., "Bureau of Justice Statistics, A National Assessment of Public Defender Office Caseloads", Justice Research and Statistics Association

Annual Meeting, October 28, 2010, www.jrsa.org/events/conferences
/presentations-10/Donald_Farole.pdf

[146] The percentage of crimes that have been solved.

[147] Tina Hotton Mahony and John Turner, "Police-reported clearance rates in Canada, 2010", Statistics Canada – Catalogue no. 85-002-X, Juristat, June, 2012.

[148] "Crime in the United States 2012", FBI: UCR, https://ucr.fbi.gov/crime-in-the-u.s/2012/crime-in-the-u.s.-2012/offenses-known-to-law-enforcement/clearances

[149] Dreisinger, *Incarceration Nations*, 2016, Chapter 6.

[150] Four additional observations and two additional recommendations are presented in this chapter of *The Costly U.S. Prison System.*

[151] Seena Fazel and Achim Wolf, "A Systematic Review of Criminal Recidivism Rates Worldwide: Current Difficulties and Recommendations for Best Practices", *Plos One* 6/18/2015; journals.plos.org/plosone/article?id=10.1371/journal.pone.0130390

[152] Excerpt from Chapter 4 of Brakke, *The Costly U.S. Prison System.*

[153] Two additional observations and three additional recommendations are presented in this chapter of *The Costly U.S. Prison System.*

[154] Excerpt from Chapter 5 of Brakke, *The Costly U.S. Prison System.*

[155] President George W. Bush, 2004 State of the Union Address

[156] Kerik, *From Jailer to Jailed,* p. 51.

[157] Ryan King, "Prison Growth," *Ohio State University News*, August 22, 2016, https://news.osu.edu/news/2016/08/22/prison-growth

[158] "Evidence Based Practice to Reduce Recidivision," Crime and Justice Institute, 2012. http://www.nationaltasc.org/wp-content/uploads/2012/11/Evidence-Based-Practice-to-Reduce-Recidivism-Crime-and-Justice-Institute-NIC.pdf

[159] "Evidence Based Practice to Reduce Recidivision," Crime and Justice Institute, 2012. http://www.nationaltasc.org/wp-content/uploads/2012/11/Evidence-Based-Practice-to-Reduce-Recidivism-Crime-and-Justice-Institute-NIC.pdf

[160] John Pfaff, *Locked In*, 2017, pp 39-40.

[161] Pfaff, *Locked In,* 2017, pp 39-40.

[162] National Institute of Justice, "Research on Reentry and Employment", https://www.nij.gov/topics/corrections/reentry/pages/employment.aspx

[163] National Institute of Justice, "Research on Reentry and Employment", https://www.nij.gov/topics/corrections/reentry/pages/employment.aspx

[164] John Pfaff, *Locked In*, 2017, pp 39-40

[165] Brakke, *The Costly U.S. Prison System*, pp. 130-131.

[166] a quarter of our current costs, if we managed to close a quarter of our prisons

[167] Lois M. Davis, Robert Bozick, Jennifer Steele, Jessica Saunders and Jeremy Miles,"Education and Vocational Training in Prisons Reduces Recidivism, Improves Job Outlook", RAND, News Release 8/22/2013, http://www.rand.org/news/press/2013/08/22.html

[168] American Civil Liberties Union

[169] Take the example of Pro-Life and Pro-Choice. I have little doubt that many Pro-Life, anti-abortion advocates are in favor of the death penalty, while Pro-Choice abortion advocates willing to terminate fetuses are unwilling to support the death penalty for murderers.

[170] Three additional recommendations are presented in this chapter of *The Costly U.S. Prison System*.

Chapter 6

[171] Excerpt from Chapter 6 of Brakke, *The Costly U.S. Prison System*.

[172] Jeremy Travis, Bruce Western and Steve Redburn, Editors, *The Growth of Incarceration in the United States: Exploring Causes and Consequences*, National Academies Press, 2014, Figure 11-1

[173] Dagan and Telles, *Prison Break*, Oxford University Press, 2016.

[174] Pfaff, *Locked In*, 2017, pp. 168-171.

[175] Ibid., pp. 161, 182, 217.

[176] Ibid., p. 169.

[177] Ibid., pp. 163-166.

[178] Pfaff, *Locked In*, 2017, pp. 194-196.

[179] "Hawaii's Opportunity Probation with Enforcement (HOPE) Program", Coalition for Evidence-Based Policy Newsletter Summary, 2/2011; http://evidencebasedprograms.org/wp-content/uploads/2012/12/HOPE-Program-Feb-2011.pdf

[180] "Swift, Certain, and Fair (SCF) Supervision Program – Including Project HOPE FY 2017 Competitive Grant Announcement", U.S. Department of Justice ,Office of Justice Programs, Bureau of Justice Assistance,1/19/2017; https://www.bja.gov/funding/SCF17.pdf

[181] Kerik, *From Jailer to Jailed*, p. 262.

[182] "Unnecessarily Incarcerated," Brennan Center, https://www.brennancenter.org/sites/default/files/publications/Unnecessarily_In carcerated.pdf

[183] Two additional recommendations are presented in this chapter of *The Costly U.S. Prison System*.

[184] Pfaff, *Locked In*, 2017, pp. 137, 154-156, 207.

[185] James Forman, Jr., "Justice Springs Eternal", *New York Times*, 3/25/17

[186] Four additional recommendations are presented in this chapter of *The Costly U.S. Prison System*.

[187] Pfaff, *Locked In*, 2017, p. 224.

[188] Pfaff, *Locked In*, 2017, p. 217.

[189] Pfaff, *Locked In*, 2017, pp. 163-166, 210-211.

[190] ACLU Campaign for Smart Justice, "Selling off Our Freedom: How Insurance Corporations Have Taken Over Our Bail System", May 2017, p. 2.

[191] Ibid., p. 9.

[192] A 2014 survey of 17 jail systems in 10 states reporting their costs found the average cost per year per jailed person was $26,098, varying from county to county even within states from a low of $17,382 (Cherokee Cty, GA) to a high of $79,555 (Onondaga Cty, NY-which includes Syracuse); The Price of Jails: Measuring the Taxpayer Cost of Local Incarceration; Vera Institute of Justice, May 2015.

[193] This is one of four recommendations made in this section of the chapter of *The Costly U.S. Prison System.*

[194] as I previously recommended in *American Justice?*

[195] Anne Kim, "Time to Abolish Cash Bail. It doesn't keep dangerous criminals off the streets. It just keeps the poor in jail—and finance companies rolling in profits", *Washington Monthly*, January/February 2017; https://washingtonmonthly.com/magazine/januaryfebruary-2017/time-to-abolish-cash-bail/

[196] Three additional recommendations are presented in this chapter of *The Costly U.S. Prison System.*

[197] Many other additional recommendations are presented in this chapter of *The Costly U.S. Prison System.*

[198] Excerpt from Chapter 7 of Brakke, *Fixing the U.S. Criminal Justice System.* Other prescriptions are to be found in Chapter 7 of the current book and in Chapter 7 of *Fixing the U.S. Criminal Justice System.*

[199] Eric Pilch, "Criminal Injustice," *Counterpoint: A Magazine of Politics and Culture*, April 19, 2012. http://www.counterpointmagazine.org/2012/04/19/criminal-injustice

[200] James Webb http://parade.com/104193/senatorjimwebb/its-time-to-change-the-law/ http://parade.com/104227/senatorjimwebb/why-we-must-fix-our-prisons

[201] http://www.humanejustice.org/background_criminal_justice.htm

[202] http://sentencing.typepad.com/sentencing_law_and_policy/2011/10/senate-republicans-block-jim-webbs-bill-for-creating-national-criminal-justice-commission.html

[203] Jess Bravin, "Two Supreme Court Justices Say Criminal-Justice System Isn't Working," *The Wall Street Journal*, March 24, 2015.

[204] Charles G. Koch and Mark V. Holden, "The Overcriminalization of America. How to reduce poverty and improve race relations by rethinking our justice system." *Politico Magazine*, January 7, 2015.

http://www.politico.com/magazine/story/2015/01/overcriminalization-of-america-113991.html#.VXXcU03bKUk

[205] Jordan Richardson, "Shining a Light on Overcriminalization", The Heritage Foundation, June 1, 2015; http://www.heritage.org/research/reports/2015/06/shining-a-light-on-overcriminalization

[206]http://www.lee.senate.gov/public/index.cfm/2015/2/lee-durbin-introduce-smarter-sentencing-act-of-2015

[207] http://www.paul.senate.gov/?p=press_release&id=1192

[208] Marc Mauer and David Cole, "How to Lock Up Fewer People," *New York Times*, May 24, 2015.

[209] Michelle Alexander, "Go to Trial: Crash the Justice System," *The New York Times*, Sunday Review, The Opinion Pages, March 10, 2012; http://tinyurl.com/avo9rjb

[210] Excerpt from Chapter 9 of Brakke, *The Price of Justice in America*.

[211] United States Department of Labor, Bureau of Labor Statistics, 2018.

[212] QuickStats: Age-Adjusted Homicide Rates, by Race/Ethnicity — National Vital Statistics System, United States, 2015–2016. MMWR Morb Mortal Wkly Rep 2018;67:462. DOI: http://dx.doi.org/10.15585/mmwr.mm6715a8.

[213] Statista, the Statistics Portal, Number of murder victims in the United States in 2017, by race/ethnicity and gender.

Chapter 7

[214] Excerpt from Chapter 7 of Brakke, *Dealing with Crime by Illegal Immigrants and the Opioid Crisis*.

[215] "Drug War Statistics," Accessed 3/15/18. http://www.drugpolicy.org/issues/drug-war-statistics

[216] Maria LeMagna, "The Opioid Epidemic Is Costing the U.S. More than $500 Billion Per Year," *MarketWatch,* March 11, 2018. https://www.marketwatch.com/story/how-much-the-opioid-epidemic-costs-the-us-2017-10-27

[217] Ibid.

[218] Butt T., Reviewed the Richard N. Fogoros, M.D., "The Cost of Drug Use to Society," Verywellmind.com, January 10, 2018. https://www.verywellmind.com/what-are-the-costs-of-drug-abuse-to-society-63037

[219] Ibid.

[220] Josh Katz, "Drug Deaths in America Are Rising Faster than Ever," *New York Times*, June 5, 2017. https://www.nytimes.com/interactive/2017/06/05/upshot/opioid-epidemic-drug-overdose-deaths-are-rising-faster-than-ever.html

[221] Katz.

[222] Katz.

[223] Excerpt from Chapter 7 of Brakke, *Dealing with Crime by Illegal Immigrants and the Opioid Crisis.*

[224] Excerpt from Chapters 8-9 of Brakke, *Dealing with Crime by Illegal Immigrants and the Opioid Crisis.*

[225] "Death Penalty Database," Cornell Center on the Death Penalty Worldwide, https://www.deathpenaltyworldwide.org/country-search-post.cfm?country=Singapore

[226] "Singapore: Executions Continue in Flawed Attempt to Tackle Drug Crime, Despite Limited Reforms," *Amnesty International,* October 11, 2017. http://www.amnesty.org/en/latest/news/2017/singapore-executions-continue-in-flawed-attempt-to-tackle-drug-crime

[227] Benjamin Haas, "Thousands in China Watch as 10 People Sentenced to Death in Sport Stadium," *The Guardian,* December 17, 2017. https://www.theguardian.com/world/2017/dec/18/thousands-china-watch-executed-sport-stadium

[228] Excerpt from Chapter 10 of Brakke, *Dealing with Crime by Illegal Immigrants and the Opioid Crisis.*

[229] "Drug Overdose Death Data," Centers for Disease Control and Prevention," https://www.cdc.gov/drugoverdose/data/statedeaths.html

[230] Holly Hedegaard, M.D., Margaret Warner, Ph.D., and Arialdi M. Miniño, M.P.H., "Drug Overdose Deaths in the United States, 1999–2016," NCHS Data Brief, No. 294, December 2017. .https://www.cdc.gov/nchs/data/databriefs/db294.pdf

[231] "Overdose Death Rates," National Institute for Drug Abuse, September 2017. https://www.drugabuse.gov/related-topics/trends-statistics/overdose-death-rates

[232] Ibid.

[233] Ibid. https://www.drugabuse.gov/related-topics/trends-statistics/overdose-death-rates

[234] "Got Pot Pledge from Trump, Senator Says," *Arkansas Democrat-Gazette,* 4/14/2018.

[235] Abigail Geiger, "About Six-in-Ten Americans Support Marijuana Legalization," FactTank, News in the Numbers, Pew Research Center, January 5, 2018. http://www.pewresearch.org/fact-tank/2018/01/05/americans-support-marijuana-legalization; Tom Angell, "Poll: Legal Marijuana Support at Record High in U.S.," October 25, 2017, Washington: Beltway Brief, Forbes.com https://www.forbes.com/sites/tomangell/2017/10/25/poll-legal-marijuana-support-at-record-high-in-u-s/#1ffd807843ff

[236] Excerpt from Chapter 11 of Brakke, *Dealing with Crime by Illegal Immigrants and the Opioid Crisis.*

[237] In making this recommendation, I acknowledge that I am a researcher at a biomedical institution, but I suggest these strategies solely as a concerned citizen. My own research has nothing to do with addiction.

[238] Excerpt from Chapter 1 of Brakke, *Fixing the U.S. Criminal Justice System.*

[239] https://static.prisonpolicy.org/scans/vera/the-price-of-prisons.pdf

[240] James Webb, "What's Wrong with Our Prisons?" *Parade,* March 29, 2009, p. 5.

[241] Excerpt from Chapter 11 of Brakke, *The Price of Justice in America.*

[242] Excerpt from Chapter 7 of Brakke, *Fixing the U.S. Criminal Justice System.*

[243] http://www.drugsense.org/cms/wodclock

[244] "Drug Addiction, Crime or Disease?" Interim and Final Reports of the Joint Committee of the American Bar Association and the American Medical Association on Narcotic Drugs, 1961, http://www.druglibrary.org/schaffer/library/studies/dacd/appendixa_9.htm

[245] "Drug Addiction, Crime or Disease?" Interim and Final Reports of the Joint Committee of the American Bar Association and the American Medical Association on Narcotic Drugs, 1961, http://www.druglibrary.org/schaffer/library/studies/dacd/appendixa_9.htm

[246] "NIDA Announces Recommendations to Treat Drug Abusers, Save Money and Reduce Crime," *NIH News,* July 24, 2006; http://www.nih.gov/news/pr/jul2006/nida-24.htm

[247] "Principles of Drug Abuse Treatment for Criminal Justice Populations – A Research-Based Guide," National Institute of Drug Abuse, National Institutes of Health, http://tinyurl.com/bc5aco9

[248] "Drug Facts: Treatment for Drug Abusers in the Criminal Justice System," Revised July 2006, http://tinyurl.com/by8kb7p

[249] "Drug Court Helps Addicts Kick Habit – and Charges," *San Francisco Chronicle,* November 12, 2012, pp. A1, A9, http://www.sfgate.com/crime/article/Drug-court-Addicts-kick-habit-charges-4028550.php

[250] San Francisco Collaborative Courts, *Research Review,* May 2009.

[251] State of New Jersey, Office of the Public Defender, http://www.state.nj.us/defender/drugcrt.shtml

[252] John Rodor, Wendy Townsend, and Avinash Sing Bhati: "Recidivism Rates for Drug Court Graduates: Nationally Based Estimates, Final Report," July, 2003. https://www.ncjrs.gov/pdffiles1/201229.pdf

[253] Nicholas Kristof, "How to Win a War on Drugs. Unlike the United States, Portugal treats addiction as a medical problem, not a criminal justice issue," *New York Times,* Sept. 24, 2017.

[254] Excerpt from Chapter 7 of Brakke, *Fixing the U.S. Criminal Justice System.*

[255] Kevin Litman-Navarro, *Marijuana legalization 2018: What States Have Decriminalized Weed*, 4/19/2018, https://www.inverse.com/article/43901-decriminalized-weed-states-2018

[256] "The Drug War Clock," citing Uniform Crime Reports, Federal Bureau of Investigation," http://www.drugsense.org/cms/wodclock

[257] Ibid.

[258] "The End of the War on Marijuana," November 9, 2012. http://www.cnn.com/2012/11/08/opinion/roffman-pot-legalization/index.html

[259] Colby Itkowitz, The Washington Post, "Senate sends opioids package to Trump", *Arkansas Democrat-Gazette*, October 4, 2018.

Chapter 8

[260] Excerpt from Preface to Brakke, *The Great National Divides*.

[261] Excerpt from Chapter 1 of Brakke, *The Great National Divides*.

[262] Photo courtesy of Our Confederate Heroes: http://www.ourconfederateheros.org/wpcontent/uploads/2012/11/Major-Battles.jpg

[263] http://www.telegraph.co.uk/news/worldnews/northamerica/usa/8319858/Abraham-Lincoln-wanted-to-deport-slaves-to-new-colonies.html

[264] Excerpt from Chapter 2 of Brakke, *The Great National Divides*.

[265] http://www.prb.org/pdf10/single-motherfamilies.pdf

[266] Alan Blinder, "Michael Slager, Officer in Walter Scott shooting, Gets 20—Year Sentence", *New York Times*, 12/7/2017.

[267] Don Babwin and Michael Tarm, "Chicago officer convicted in killing of teen", Associated Press, *Arkansas Democrat-Gazette*, 10/6/2018.

[268] Four additional suggested solutions are presented in this chapter of *The Great National Divides.*

[269] Excerpt from Chapter 3 of Brakke, *The Great National Divides*.

[270] Excerpt from Chapter 4 of Brakke, *The Great National Divides*.

[271] Excerpt from Chapter 5 of Brakke, *The Great National Divides*.

[272] Excerpt from Chapter 6 of Brakke, *The Great National Divides*.

[273] Colin Woodard, *American Nations: A History of the Eleven Rival Cultures of North America,* 2011.

[274] https://www.psychologytoday.com/blog/evolution-the-self/201210/greed-the-ultimate-addiction

[275] http://www.huffingtonpost.com/dr-tian-dayton/money-addiction_b_221937.html

[276] https://www.forbes.com/sites/davidmarotta/2013/02/28/dwight-d-eisenhower-on-tax-cuts-and-a-balanced-budget/#7d4950115047

[277] Excerpt from Chapter 7 of Brakke, *The Great National Divides*.

[278] Benjy Egel, "California now world's fifth largest economy, bigger than Britain", *Sacramento Bee*, 5/4/2018.

[279] "New American Civil War? Some people think it's already begun", *rt.com*, 6/26/2018. https://www.rt.com/usa/430957-america-new-civil-war-trump/

[280] Amy Guttman and Dennis Thompson, *The Spirit of Compromise. Why Governing Demands It and Campaigning Undermines It*, Princeton University Press, 2012.

[281] Ibid.

[282] Mickey Edwards, *The Parties Versus the People: How to Turn Republicans and Democrats into Americans,* Yale University Press, 2013.

[283] Colby Itkowitz, The Washington Post, "Senate sends opioids package to Trump", *Arkansas Democrat-Gazette*, October 4, 2018.

[284] http://www.ncsl.org/research/fiscal-policy/supermajority-vote-requirements-to-pass-the-budget635542510.aspx